How I survived as a young

beyond
ᴛʜᴇbreakpoint

DEBBIE FARIS

RIVERSTONE GROUP
PUBLISHING

dedication

To Randy,

It was an amazing ride. It was my privilege to be your choice and your love. Thank you for coming into my life and for creating enough memories to humble me, to carry forward and to cherish.

Always and forever,

[signature]

acknowledgements

*M*any people have contributed to this journey of becoming a reluctant author. Some were cheerleaders or gave me a gentle push. Others took the time to read my early manuscript and offer their insights. However, there is a special person I must single out. Without her valuable editorial input, spot-on insight, and incisive probing, this book would be considerably lessened. I am deeply thankful and incredibly indebted to my dear friend, Laurie Curreri. Partnering with both Laurie and Jack Watts brought *Beyond the Breakpoint* to its fullest fruition and potential.

Riverstone Group Publishing
ISBN: 978-1-7346235 4-3

contents

"Dear Lord, please, PLEASE: only give me what I can handle tomorrow"

I should have been screaming this prayer, but I was beyond the boundaries of physical exhaustion and emotional depletion. Lacking the strength to say anything out loud, it was little less than a mere whisper as I crawled into bed. Randy was lying diagonally so I only had a tiny triangle of space left to lie down. It did not matter, I am a little person, whatever was fine. Have you ever fallen asleep before you close your eyes? Is it even possible? Perhaps. I don't remember closing mine and I was out like a light before my head settled into the pillow.

One month prior, on the eve of Thanksgiving, I found my husband in our garage. He was weak and immobile with a cut above his eyebrow. As usual, he tried to brush it off and just wanted help getting into bed. This was not the first time had I found him on the ground or passed out, so I was not alarmed, angry, or even disappointed. Life had already taught me those hard lessons and these emotions did not rear their ugly head. Instead, I donned the familiar mantle of levity and tried to reason so he would get some stitches. As my logic intersected with his blankness, I began to have the deep conviction this situation was very different. Something was seriously wrong.

With the kind of strength that a lioness reserves for her cubs I hauled him into the car and raced off to the local hospital. How I accomplished that remains a mystery because I'm a waif-like Chinese woman with virtually no upper body strength. My arms are like sticks and my hands are very small. Randy was 5'10", slim and fit, but his greater weight and lack of cooperation should have made that feat impossible. Somehow, I accomplished the task. As the day unfolded, what I thought were going to be a couple of stitches turned into kidney failure, a compromised liver, potential lung cancer and a plethora of tests that spanned over a two-week stay. At the onset he was blissfully unaware of all that was wrong with his internal systems but as he regained strength, this hospitalization quickly turned into his personal nightmare and my version of a horrible melodrama.

As the situation unfolded I was burning the candle on both ends, desperately trying to maintain a normal routine for my 8 and 10-year-old boys and care for the baby who was two years old. Between their school, naps and bedtime, I frantically raced back and forth to the hospital to spend every moment possible with Randy and the doctors. Each time we conferred, they would deliver the news of another major organ issue. My emotions migrated from perplexed apprehension to heightened alertness and then sank into emotional numbness. The status of his health was going from awful to worse and my mind could not absorb the implications. I felt my brain was going to explode when in fact it was teetering on the verge of collapsing.

While my inner self was struggling to remain collected, I was equally falling apart on the outside. You could see it in my face. Even though I had given birth to three boys, I was slender, retaining the same figure I had prior to the babies. How I stayed trim had nothing to do with will-power or workouts. I was simply blessed with awesome genes and a rapid metabolism. My wardrobe was a form of expression so more often than not, I could pull myself together as stylish mom chic: practical put together. This situation was completely undoing me both inside and out. I never left home plain-faced, but makeup could not disguise the harrowed look that was starting to etch itself on my countenance. We had already lived through the experiences of an overdose, detoxes and rehabs so I was a seasoned crisis manager. I had nerves of steel and could be eerily calm and collected when faced with pressure, but this hole was leaking faster than I could plug my boat. I was steering a sinking vessel headed into uncharted waters without the least idea how to be a captain.

In caring for Randy, I was also managing his growing desperation to leave the hospital. He was looking for the way out while I cajoled him to remain hospitalized and patient to the relentless rounds of nurses, blood taking, and invasive tests. If you have ever experienced a prolonged hospital stay, you realize that the monotony is far from restful. The boredom is pierced with the cold smell of sterility, the unwelcome beeping of alarms and the perfunctory nurse visits that are anything but entertaining.

In the beginning, his health was so tenuous the doctors and I decided to remain silent about the possibility of cancer, even though all the indicators were pointing in this direction. We thought it was best not to unduly alarm Randy. As we discussed each new set of exploratory tests, I danced around the real issue while putting on the façade of positivity and calmness. It was imperative for him to stay in the hospital so that we could get to the bottom of his health conundrum. If he self-discharged, his insurance might not cover the costly tests at a later date. It felt like I was holding him back with threadbare gauze while he was trying to run away, all along harboring the fear of the unthinkable and knowing there was nowhere for me to escape.

In an effort to comprehend how my world was falling apart, I became intent on deciphering the implications of my husband's health issues. An engineer by trade, my training taught me to identify cause and effect, to think methodically, and to be efficient. It was my second nature to look for solutions, figure out implementation and plan for alternate scenarios. This thought process was my driver as the crisis unfolded. Others might have been blissfully shocked or catatonic but my go to mode has always been to do, to move, to act. Unable to sleep, late night I googled all of the new terms, symptoms and diagnostics I had overheard during the day, trying to figure out the normal ranges of enzymes, the definition of rhabdomyolysis, what in the world is a guided needle biopsy ... Overwhelmed, it was like taking a crash course in a new language when going to a foreign country I never wished to visit.

For very different reasons, the hospital stay was traumatic for both of us. As a visual artist and outdoorsman, being confined to the sterile and institutional environment of a hospital room was horrific to him. Randy could not sleep in peace and when awake, he was living out his worst fears. Smart and streetwise, once he was stabilized it did not take him long to figure out that something was terribly wrong. As the seriousness of this predicament sank in and he faced the possibility of cancer, my challenge morphed from keeping him willingly hospitalized to uplifting his spirits and nurturing his faith. In my case, I was stretched beyond anything I had ever experienced trying to support my husband, be present for my three sons and remain capable to deal with the medical decisions. I fervently prayed for strength to avert caving into the fear and despair that were ever present.

He was finally discharged just in time for Christmas. Considering it all, we had a beautiful, albeit quiet holiday because he was very, very weak after a lung biopsy and all the trauma to his body. Randy was elated when the lung spots turned out to be histoplasmosis, caused by a fungus he must have acquired while he trekked around the world. As an advertising photographer, his work took him to fabulously glamorous locations like Paris, Prague or London but he was a photo journalist at heart and his early career days were scattered with visits to exotic and far flung locations such as Morocco, India and Egypt. Back in the day when adventure travel had yet to become a coined phrase, he was already seeking the undiscovered and exploring off the beaten paths. Perhaps it was then that the fungus had nestled in his lungs.

These spores are typically present in the droppings of bats and birds. Somewhere, somehow, he had inhaled them as he traversed the country and circled the globe in pursuit of his craft. The fungus caused the lung nodules, but histoplasmosis was a treatable condition. Randy was reserved by nature and not one to dwell on bad news. Because I'd personally witnessed his incredible ability to deny the most obvious truths, I was surprised to see how much he had internalized the terrible possibility of cancer. I was not expecting to see him so visibly relieved to have dodged this bullet. For the first time, he was actually the more grounded of the two of us when facing our new reality. On the other hand, I was exhausted from being everything to everyone and wondered how I'd find the stamina to manage the next round of doctors but at least, Now We Knew.

I think one of the worst moments in times of crisis is the endless waiting while facing the unknown. The being in limbo without any of control over yours or your loved one's destiny while thoughts assault you with unfathomable variations of the worst-case scenario. When there is a set of instructions or a plan to follow, I believe it's human nature to find comfort in the known, in the notion of control. This is such a fallacy because we never really know what curveballs the future will fling but the illusion is welcome because it keeps hope alive and despair at bay.

13

Personally, I was incapable of feeling anything, even gratitude for a plan. I suppose this was self-preservation, knowing that some part of me had to remain functional and alive so I could continue to care for our family. My friends would describe me as a highly intelligent, social type A personality (their words, not mine) with an open heart and always a smile on my face. They would say I was a caring listener, able to be present in the moment and thoughtfully connect. A multitasker to a fault, I was a critical thinker and was always conjuring up some fun idea. I used all of these abilities to hold our life together and move us forward, but the experience of the last year and the nightmare of the past month left me emotionally spent and physically exhausted. I was but a shell of that capable and reliable woman. Neither could I fathom how I would keep all the balls in the air. Always, in the back of my mind lurked the nagging question that remained unanswered: What caused the original fall? What if it was not the histoplasmosis but something else?

As we wrapped up his hospital stay, I pleaded for answers from the doctors but the best the nephrologist flippantly remarked was "We are not CSI". I was incredulous. How could this be the answer of a doctor? What do you mean by "you're not sure"? How will I know this won't happen again? "Oh, you'll know, you'll see it coming." Really? Are. You. Serious. You mean you are a DOCTOR but don't have a definite explanation? As I interrogated him, I must have seemed insignificant and one his many rounds for the day, but the job in front of me was overwhelming and life altering. It was up to me ask the questions and deal with the ramifications because I was the one charting all of the critical paths and also executing the action plan. I felt like I was the pilot, purser and deckhand of a boat that was sailing upwind. This mothership must not go down. It can't.

All of these mental gyrations were sapping what little emotional strength I had left, and fear gripped my heart. I feared for my boys, for our future, for our family. The success of our company, Randy Faris Photography, totally relied on his talent. It had been years since I left my executive life in corporate America, so he was our only breadwinner. After all of the peaks and valleys that life had provided thus far, I just wanted a normal, stable and predictable existence. With his success, Randy took me along for an unbelievable joyride, but I would have longingly embraced boring, mundane, and uneventful because life in the last few years had been anything but that.

As 2009 came to an end, December 30th found Randy incoherent and glazed. His weak body was present, but his mind was not. My first clue was that his sparkling hazel-green eyes were lackluster and vacant. We were supposed to take a cruise in a few days and I could not risk his being sick in the middle of the Caribbean. Remembering the callous remarks of the discharging nephrologist saying "Oh, you'll see it coming again", I feared we were once more headed to the vortex. I dropped our New Year's Eve preparations and rushed him back to the hospital. Randy did not know who was the US President (Obama) nor the name of our first son (David). As I sat, feeling cold and miserable in the ER, I waited, wondered and re-lived the prior month's nightmare. All of the emotions associated with his first stay started to percolate and surface. Whatever semblance of normalcy that the past two weeks had afforded quickly dissipated and was replaced by the draining and depleting thoughts of facing the unknown. Again.

After a brain scan and some other tests, the hospital staff deemed appropriate to release him. Randy had such bad recollection of his recent stay that he was desperate to leave the ER. An earlier version of myself would have insisted on having more concrete answers but I was so exhausted that all I wanted to hear was good news. Despite falling short of a clear explanation for his confusion and memory loss, I acquiesced to both Randy and the hospital staff, and we headed back home. Thankfully my parents were visiting so they were in charge of the three boys … one less worry. I took inventory of the household, made something to eat for Randy and headed to our bedroom to feed him.

The past month ordeal had taken its toll on him and he was SO thin. Gaunt and pallid he looked more like a character from a Tim Burton film than the man I married. He had lost so much weight, was colorless and the sparkle in his eyes was but a vague recollection. He used to be strong and was handsome to me. The quintessential cool California surfer dude, he was also the type of guy that could make most women feel at ease because he was gentle, unassuming and sensitive. It was my mission to make him eat and breathe life back into him even if I had to spoon feed him one soft noodle at a time.

He was an all American: somewhat German, part English, perhaps Irish with a trace of Cherokee somewhere up the line. Meanwhile I was 100 percent ethnically Chinese. We looked so different but at that moment we were equally haggard, drained and grey. After being together for 20 years, we did not have to verbally communicate. He could read me like a book and must have seen my emotional defeat while I battled his physical demise. He knew I was losing it, that I had reached the end of my rope as the game changer, the manager, the nurse and the mother. Witnessing my exhaustion and the despair etched in my features he said "Deb, don't worry. Everything will be all right." Always the eternal optimist.

I wish I had given more value to the optimism Randy had about any situation. Certainly, my pragmatic realism was not of any help because it mired me in the very real implications of his illness and did not allow me to see past my own challenges. My personal well of strength was running dry and my ability to be tender, loving and patient was dwindling in the process. I had reverted to my default mode: doing rather than feeling.

"Dear Lord, please, PLEASE, only give me what I can handle tomorrow" I prayed crawling into bed that night. I woke up the next morning and he looked so peaceful. He had not moved an inch. I gazed at his face, he had beautiful eye lashes, long and curly. I touched him gently, so he'd know that I was getting out of bed. He was very still, eerily still. I pulled away the bedsheets and observed the color surrounding the lung biopsy wounds was a mottled, unhealthy purple. Again, I touched him and he did not stir. Neither did I see him breathing but this did not register, I just knew that something was terribly wrong. I rushed to wake up my dad who fumbled out of bed and went to check our bedroom while I called 911. That was my last clear memory of December 31, 2009. After, it was all a blur.

The paramedics arrived almost instantly. They went into our bedroom and minutes later gently announced that Randy had died in his sleep several hours ago, there was nothing to be done. I was numb. Somehow the police also arrived. They interviewed me and I mechanically recounted the events of the last 24 hours. I was still in shock. I did not know who told my oldest child, 10-year-old David, but I heard him sobbing loudly in the next room. I could not even move to comfort him, I just wanted to be alone, but the tears were not yet forthcoming. I called Amy, my bestie. We had shared crisis after crisis and were bonded by all that we had lived through together. She was my first and my only call. After her, I finally arrived at breakpoint, crumbled apart and started sobbing. "Is this Your answer to my prayer? Death? Is death what I can handle today?" I felt like screaming but strength was but a distant memory, so I whispered "Lord, really? ... Really?"

The notion that I was a 41-year old widow and that my 3 sons were fatherless did not even enter my reality at that moment. All I could feel was the utter sense of devastation as a terrible loneliness enveloped me.

17

Any of the fears that I had previously felt dissipated and were replaced by emptiness, anguish and infinite sorrow. I did not realize that a part of me had also died with him and life as I had known it would never be the same.

Sons of the Good Earth

"The journey of a thousand miles starts with a single step."

Lao Tzu - Chinese Philosopher and Writer

Equally terrified and elated, the boy darted away from the walled village. The moonlight illuminated the dips, rocks and shrubs in his path as he made his way through central China's rough terrain. Kung Kung was leaving behind all he ever knew, even the coolie queue braid that he and cousin Lee hacked off before venturing onto the treacherous roads that lead to Kowloon. Wanting to blend in with other travelers, the braid would have been a dead giveaway about the peasants they were. This was the early 1900s and their village had heard the tales of gold and fortune found in California, located on the other side of the world. Nonetheless, the next adventure lay in a strange narrow strip of land named Panama, where it was said the Americans were carving a path that would unite two vast oceans.

Kung Kung's mother was a minor wife. As such, she was only too aware of the opportunities lacking for both her and her only son. The walls that surrounded their village did nothing to shield her from the misery and hunger that were her lot in life. Worse yet, she imagined that her precious boy could end up as a victim of the revolution that was sweeping the land. She was uneducated and simple, limited in her worldview, but her mother's heart yearned for something better than what was her reality.

Somehow, she managed to convince Lee to take Kung Kung with him as he departed for adventure and a new life across the ocean. The boy was barely twelve years old, perhaps even younger, but he was strong, obedient, and hardworking. As she said goodbye to her only child, she managed to squash the foreboding sensation of infinite loss that was building in her chest.

Instead, she said pragmatically, "Remember to think of me. Remember to send me money when you get rich."

The boy was too young and excited to realize he would never see his mother again and she was too much too practical of a Hakka woman to let her feelings take hold, much less allow them to show up as a weakness. Her lot in life was do or die. Hakka women have always been known to be strong and fierce mothers. She was no exception to her genetic code.

Almost a century later, when my grandfather experienced the last sunset of his life, despite having a wise and beloved wife, six offspring and seventeen grandchildren, the final words he spoke would be those to beseech the presence of his Mama. He had not seen her for over eighty-five years. Yet, when he died, she was on his mind.

This is the indelible mark some mothers have the power to imprint on their children. It is both a blessing and a burden.

Motherhood is the salient factor that has also determined my life choices, both before the tragedy and then with singular purpose in the last decade since it all happened. This is the story of what I have done because of my sons, along with some of the lessons I have learned traversing the not so straight path of my journey from mourning to joy.

The Way We Were

"Give a bowl of rice to a man and you fill feed him for a day.
Teach him how to grow his own rice and you will save his life."

Kǒng Fūzǐ - Chinese Philosopher
- also known to the West as Confucius.

Although I have been known to frantically search for my eyeglasses while they are sitting atop my head, I still remember what I was wearing on the last day I was naively and blissfully happy. It is curious how we retain some memories while others elude us. A periwinkle purple, white flowered, shapeless Hawaiian muumuu covered my seven-month baby bump. I was so slender that I looked like a pregnant sardine. From behind I looked normal but sideways one could imagine that I had swallowed a basketball. The tent of a dress was as expansive and cheerful as my life: I was happily married, waiting for my hubby to return from an exciting photo assignment and we were expecting our first baby … The baby that might hopefully close the rift between my mother and Randy. The makings of that rift were the first emotional storm that unhinged my world and rocked my boat. After many a prayer for guidance and with the buoyant optimism of youth, I set my compass north, took a deep breath, and married the love of my life.

If opposites attract, we were that textbook couple. East meets West. A Chinese-Hispanic first daughter and the All-American last child. I, the engineer who loved art and was soaring in the corporate manufacturing world. He, the artist who was brilliantly technical and was equally rising as a professional photographer. Although I had shown artistic promise as a child, I was just as proficient in math and science. Being a third generation Chinese, my career choices were narrowed down to practical professions that could secure meaningful employment such as the medical arts, law or engineering.

Why are Chinese so universally driven to excel educationally? I suppose the origins of my story might explain that question. Branches of my ancestry trace back over a thousand years, as an ancient group of people from the Middle Kingdom began their exodus to the valleys of southern China, fleeing the Tartars, war and famine. These "guest people," known as the Hakka, settled in the highlands and did not intermarry with their lowland neighbors. They stubbornly kept their customs, language, and identity intact for centuries.

Hakka women were known to be uniquely determined, intelligent and strong willed. Refusing to have their feet bound (as was decreed by law), they worked the fields alongside the men, and they were resolutely independent. In seventeenth century China, a tiny-footed, idle wife was the portrait of gentility. Their hesitant balancing baby steps were considered graceful and their reliance on attendants to help them get around implied status and wealth. These notions were ridiculous to a Hakka woman: small feet prevented them from running away from raiders, climbing the hills and contributing to their household. Attendants were best used to till the land.

According to legend, Emperor Zhao Bing was so impressed by their courage and stoic bravery after they saved his life that he conferred upon all Hakka women the title of "Ju Ren" or "Wife of a Senior Official"—a title of significant respect otherwise awarded posthumously. So fierce was their reputation that lowland mothers would threaten their insolent sons, "Get off your lazy bum or I'll marry you to a Hakka girl." These women were smart, powerful and demanded an equal voice in family matters ... a dreadful prospect that no sensible man could possibly want ... as a wife.

Although the Hakka women were singularly determined and obstinate, they—along with the rest of China— experienced centuries of misery, famines and scarcity. Having a bowl of rice to feed a family equated to life. One garnished with a little meat or fat, signified wealth. To this day, "Finish your food, clean your plate" is the chant that Chinese mothers will recite to their children after each meal. This ancestral fear of starvation coupled with a system where advancement was mostly obtained by the scholarly route, caused its people to educationally excel. In a culture where survival came and went with the ebb and flow of rivers, wealth might be transitory, but knowledge remained. We were no exception to this legacy.

The aspirations that Randy and I had for our young sons were mainly driven by the benefits we both received from attending well-respected, high-level educational institutions. In my case, I ended up going to the same university as my father. He was the youngest of six siblings and the only one who went to college. Kung-Kung and Miss Marie, my paternal grandparents, owned a small grocery store. They lived in Colon, a bustling port city off Panama's Atlantic coast in Central America. When possible, my grandfather made ends meet by running gangs of workers building the Panama Canal railroad. Although they had the essentials, money was very limited. In those days, a high school diploma from St. Joseph's usually guaranteed a job in commerce, as a clerk, or as a secretary. Dad's older brothers worked and helped support their parents and the younger siblings. The funds to pursue a higher education were nonexistent and the prevailing goal was to "get a good job" after completing high school. By the time my father was of age, the notion of college as the next step had started to germinate amongst his peers, but few could afford it.

Dad, who had never set foot on a farm, studied Agronomy Engineering because the Organization of American States deemed this necessary for a developing country and a private foundation provided an all-inclusive scholarship. Although he was always a good student, maturity must have kicked in when he turned sixteen because he strove to be the top student in his final year at St. Joseph's. Falling in love with my mother also was significant because a degree was imperative if he wanted to be considered as a possible suitor. Regardless of his motivations, having perfect grades earned him the merit scholarship.

Although he was always a good student, maturity must have kicked in when he turned sixteen because he strove to be the top student in his final year at St. Joseph's.

Other than my grandmother's encouragement, no one else in his family could relate to the application process which he undertook all on his own. Such was the limited life—you seized the opportunities as they came, even if they were not your first or even any of your preferences. Education that gives life-changing opportunities was to be embraced, and it was worth the commensurate effort. My father was barely seventeen years old when he packed up, boarded his first international flight, and headed off to Mexico to broaden his horizons.

His scholarship was originally intended for a university in Puerto

Rico, but he advocated for the Monterrey Institute of Technology in Mexico. Modeled after MIT in the United States, it was founded in 1943 as a technical school to train those who would work in Mexico's burgeoning industries. Agronomy was a difficult program but again, he was at the top of his class. This distinction afforded him a second scholarship to pursue a Graduate Degree at UC Davis. Dad completed his Masters in Soils at the frenetic pace of one year—the time allotted by his employer in Panama for a leave of absence.

On the other hand, my mom grew up under significantly more privileged circumstances. She was the only child of Mike Tang, a well-liked Chinese businessman who owned a general merchandise store and several other enterprises. Her mother, Dorothy, was a beautiful, thoughtful, and devout woman. One of my earliest memories of her was praying the rosary which she did on a daily basis. Grandma's recorded impression in my baby album reads, "Debbie is a cheeky little girl" because I was bossy and demanding with her. She never said no to me and she was beloved by myself and all who knew her.

Most children in Colon were affordably educated at the Catholic schools where tuition was heavily subsidized ($2-$8 a month). At a time when few "countrymen" were involved in politics, Mike was a city councilman who sponsored several sports teams and had the means to send my mother to the American school which was considerably more expensive ($50 per month). Mom enjoyed learning to quench her intellectual curiosity. In addition to being smart, she was also musically inclined and could play the piano and a few other instruments. With her high grades, test scores and my grandfather's financial ability, it was never a question whether she would attend college. In addition, her uncle (my grandfather's only brother) had already set the standard when he graduated from NYU as one of the first Chinese dentists in Panama. I suppose my grandparents would have wanted her to study medicine, but my mother went to UC Berkley and finished her education at the University of Florida in Gainesville to become an educator. All through these years my parents kept in touch and their love remained alive until they both returned to Panama from their studies abroad.

After a few years of adult courtship, they married and moved to the province of Chiriqui which was about an 8-hour drive away from Colon. Supplying most of the cattle and produce for the country, this region was Panama's breadbasket. To this day, Chiriqui remains a proudly independent state with occasional separatist dreams as an autonomous republic. However, compared to the more sophisticated Colon, my mother must have felt like she was moving to the outback.

As the Atlantic access to the Panama Canal, the French initially settled Colon in their failed attempt to bridge the two oceans. In the late 1800's, newcomers from all corners of the globe were drawn to participate in this major world project. They came from the Caribbean Islands, Europe, China and the US, merging into a colorful and unique amalgamation that was multicultural before the term was even minted. Such was the diversity of foods and flavors that the pungent smells of curry, fried fish, beignets, garlic pa-chan kai, and ketchup laden hot dogs commonly emanated from a typical Colon kitchen of those days.

Reminiscent of the French Quarter in New Orleans, the city planners laid out an organized town with wide avenues adorned by picturesque and ornate buildings. The multitude of immigrants were housed in these buildings decorated with wide continuous porches that covered the sidewalks. The porches were more than an embellishment: they shielded the street level pedestrians from the alternating downpours or blazing sunshine in this tropical and humid latitude. As a common area, the porches also allowed the second and upper story residents to socialize amongst each other with a proximity that blurred the lines between friends and family. When the USA took over after the French fiasco, they expanded the city with more housing and development. The Americans brought their organization, sanitation principles, and their army to protect the Canal which was then considered a US territory. By the time my parents were growing up in the 1950's, Colon boasted eight movie theaters, a dance hall, a YMCA and many other amenities that graced its citizens' lives. It was a small town with a big city vibe.

My mother loved to learn and appreciated music, literature, and culture. Moving to Chiriqui must have been a far departure from all that she had known, but she also enjoyed the simplicity of nature which was abundant in that part of the country. Friendly and generous, she was one to make the best out of any circumstance and she formed lasting relationships with her new surroundings. As the manager of a large citrus processing factory and orange plantations, this was fitting employment for my father's Agronomy Engineering degree. He was an expert in his field and was excelling in his work. Nonetheless, as I neared school age and with the birth of my younger brother, they must have realized that it was time to leave this rural provincial setting to seek better education opportunities for us.

Friendly and generous, she was one to make the best out of any circumstance and she formed lasting relationships with her new surroundings.

We moved to Venezuela when my brother could barely walk, and I was 4 years old. We left behind orange groves and country life in Panama, where I spent my toddlerhood running around half naked chasing chickens and roosters. Dad had been hired by a company then owned by the Rockefeller family and he went on to forge a tremendously successful career. We settled in Valencia, the industrial capital of Venezuela and the operation center for many of the multinational and local industries. Because of his drive, wisdom and exceptional skills as an administrator, our family was able to enjoy the affluence that had eluded his ancestors. As the operations head for one of Venezuela's most iconic beverage brands, we were no strangers to the corporate jets, haciendas, country clubs, and chauffeurs that came with his executive position. His professional success also allowed my well educated and enlightened mother to stay at home and be the driving force behind my exposure to a multitude of lessons, hobbies, and refinements that life had to offer. Even though the lack of previous generations was left behind, the notion of attaining a higher education remained a cultural imperative in our household. Years later, it would be a tacit directive that permeated into my own parental philosophy when I had children of my own.

**Even though the lack of previous generations
was left behind, the notion of attaining a
higher education remained a
cultural imperative in our household.**

While the United States was mired in the oil crisis of the '70's, my family nestled in the comfortable nest of prosperity and experienced the petro-dollar in Venezuela, oil rich and famous for its beauty queens. A land of incredible beauty and mineral wealth, Venezuela was graced to the north with a Caribbean coastline, laced with turquoise clear waters and white sands. At its west is the beginning of the Andean mountain range while the other parts of the country host a variety of topographies that include dessert, rainforest and savannah. The Auyan-Tepui, an ancient granite plateau located in the remote south, boasts the highest uninterrupted waterfall on Earth. Named "Angel Falls" after Jimmy

Angel, an American adventurer who discovered it in 1937, it is nestled in a UNESCO World Heritage Site and National Park called Canaima.

Venezuela also has a temperate climate and rich fertile land that could grow and feed most anything needed for man to survive and thrive. Its stable democracy attracted many immigrants and multinational corporations, so our life was also enhanced by the many expats seeking opportunities in this land of the black gold: Italy, Spain, Brazil, Chile, Colombia, Argentina, India...we had friends from a variety of countries spanning the globe.

Venezuela's ample middle class enjoyed a standard of living that could rival or surpass any first world society of those days. Caracas, the capital, was nestled on a beautiful mountain range named "El Avila" and had the temperate climate of an eternal springtime. Valencia, where we lived, was on the warm side, fluctuating comfortably between the low 70's and mid 80's. My neighborhood was well laid out and organized, with single family homes in certain sections and high-rise condominiums in other designated areas. My school was within walking distance as was a small downtown area with a bakery, small grocery store, pharmacy, shoe shop and other businesses.

As I was growing up, Venezuela was a common tour stop for artists such as Pavarotti, Queen, The Police or Cyndy Lauper. Spring and summer fashions from Italy and Spain arrived six months earlier than in Europe because fall and winter were non-existent in the tropics. Most of our friends lived in single-family homes or spacious apartments, where both parents each had their own car, employed domestic help and sent their children to private schools. During the school year I received art, tennis, golf, horseback riding, piano and music lessons. For our summers, my parents expanded our world view traveling to Europe and the United States.

The town where we lived boasted of a multitude of social clubs that catered to the variety of its citizens. Our first membership was at the International Club, where most of the ex-pats and their families socialized. As time passed and my dad's career advanced, it became clear that they would be staying in Venezuela, and they joined a few other clubs to pursue his interest in tennis and golf. In short, we moved to a country that had it all: oil rich, favorable climate, incredible natural beauty, and a strategic location. Tragically, after the implosion of democracy from within, now this once wealthy Venezuela is but a figment of the collective imagination of those of us who experienced her in the 70's and 80's.

Since 1910, Venezuela had the most stable currency of any Latin country with the value of the Bolivar pegged at 4.30 to 1 US Dollar (Today, the currency skyrocketed into the millions but it's worthless). February 18, 1983 marked the beginning of the Latin American debt crisis with Venezuela at its forefront. My parents wisely heeded the counsel of two close friends: "Get your money out of the country." One was Cuban, the other Peruvian, and both had seen the writing on the wall—having already experienced a Latin American downturn in their own countries. Those who had never witnessed the warning signs of an imminent crisis were reluctant to contemplate such a maneuver because the rates at the local banks were extremely enticing. Most were complacent and believed the government would not take any drastic measures. I remember a flurry of activity in our household, my normally calm mother running back and forth to the banks and tense phone calls earlier in the week. On that infamous Black Friday, the government closed the banks and froze all accounts to prevent a massive currency flight. All whose money remained in Venezuela saw their savings plummet by 75% in a matter of hours … and they could do nothing about it.

**I remember a flurry of activity in our
household, my normally calm mother running
back and forth to the banks and tense
phone calls earlier in the week.**

Other than a couple thousand in the bank, the value of our home, and their club memberships, my parents transferred everything to US accounts and were spared from economic devastation. I vaguely recall the effects of this downturn because it played out gradually over the next months and years. Moreover, the adults were guarded about the implications when children were within earshot. What I did witness was the slow erosion of financial stability amongst our neighbors, quashed dreams of going abroad to study amidst my friends, and the steady rise of crime and danger in Venezuela. When we arrived in the early 70's it was not unheard of to have your car stolen, your purse snatched, or your jewelry yanked off your neck (whereas this was a rare occurrence in Panama). As the situation worsened, it became commonplace to get held-up at gunpoint in restaurants, beauty salons and even your own home. One of my classmates was fatally injured from a gunshot wound when intruders entered her house. We never learned if it was her family or the robbers who fired the gun because it was not unusual for civilians to own firearms for personal protection.

Clearly this first devaluation and the ones that cascaded afterwards were indelible, but I recall a stable and happy childhood grounded in love and discipline. I had an extraordinary father and a unique relationship with him. For example, when I was sick or had a fever nightmare, I would call out to him rather than my mother. He was also the one who would send me to the corner if I was sassy or would make a big show about rolling up the newspaper and cracking it noisily for a "pow-pow" which was our code word for a spanking. On the other hand, I was confidently the apple of his eye which he declared regularly in no uncertain terms. His secretary used to guard his time like a bulldog, but she knew to pass along any of my phone calls, regardless of where he was, who he was meeting or what he was doing. I credit his love and our relationship as crucial in developing my self-worth and confidence— attributes that became my armor when facing the battles that life would place in my path.

I credit his love and our relationship as crucial in developing my self-worth and confidence–

After a brief stint at the American School, my mother accurately foresaw that my friendships would last only as long as my classmates' parents in country assignments (the norm was usually 2 years) so she transferred me to an all-girls Catholic school. We spoke English at home, but I was educated in the exacting and grammar-perfect Castilian Spanish. Mom was somewhat wary the nuns might be overly stern and severe, but as timed passed, she noted their warmth, care and humor. I remained at St. Angel for my entire elementary and high school education. Aside from receiving a classical academic education, the pillars of my faith were built by those Spanish nuns who lovingly taught us the Gospel, encouraged mission work and expected our behavior to reflect proper Christian values.

Despite mostly receiving excellent grades, my parents never set them as an expectation. Top marks were simply the result of utilizing my abilities to their highest extent which they encouraged and supported. I recall many a high school project that required typing to which my father would sit down and hammer out a 30-page report with honed skills learned at St. Joseph's. I also credit my mom's background as an educator in understanding the importance of nurturing self-esteem and instilling the joy of learning rather than holding us hostage to a numerical grade. Even though I was doing well in math, she hired a private professor simply because he was an exceptional teacher and she wanted me to experience being tutored by a gifted educator.

No doubt my parents placed a higher value on academic achievement, but they also monitored my performance in all areas. I remember several of the non-athletic girls, including myself, failing the quarter for Volleyball PE. Without drama or hesitation, by the end of the term we had received expert coaching that allowed us to place on the varsity team. On the other hand, when my classmates elected me as their "Miss" in Sophomore year (this was Venezuela, where beauty pageant indoctrination started young and was given much importance), my parents did not show up to the homecoming festivities. "Here is your dress and let's shop for some matching shoes" was all that I recall of my mother's involvement. Although being chosen as a "Miss" was every Venezuelan little girl's secret dream, it was not a big deal to them, nor did they expect it would be for me.

In truth, I was mildly shocked to have been nominated by my class-mates. As the tally from each girl's vote accumulated on the blackboard, shock turned into momentary disbelief that I was their elected beauty queen. As a teen, I was unaware of my looks: in my mind, I was neither here nor there—just neutral. My identity was defined by my family, my behavior, and how I performed. I do not recall my parents ever commenting about my appearance except the one time my cutoff shorts were called out as inappropriate to leave the house. "Where do you think you are going dressed like that young lady?" was all my father had to say. How I presented myself mattered only in terms of being respectable for the occasion or situation. As long as I was pleasing and pleasant, I had no restrictions.

However, I was keenly aware of my ethnicity. In 1970, Valencia's population was nearly one million inhabitants with only eight Chinese families, including ours. They embraced us, but we were unable to fully communicate and integrate because we did not speak Chinese. Today, China is unified under the umbrella of Mandarin as its national language but in the pre-Mao era, Chinese was really a collection of dialects that acted as a communication barrier amongst its own people. Consequently, those who left China in the immigrant waves of the 1900's couldn't speak to each other unless they came from the same province and shared the same dialect. One could only imagine a market full of Chinese, all speaking at the same time, and no one understanding each other unless aided by a translator! When my ancestors arrived in Panama, because of the American influence in building the Canal, English was the prevailing and unifying language.

Given such few Asians in Valencia, naturally, we stood out. My father's wise advice was, "Always be aware of your behavior because you look different and everyone will remember you." As a teenager, it was not unusual to be singled out on the street by the "Hey Mamacita" catcalls which turned into derogative sing-song imitations of Chinese if I ignored the offender. Even though it was uncomfortable, I learned it was better not to respond. However, when one of my classmates slyly used racial slurs to diminish me amongst our girlfriends, I was bothered and disturbed. Much later in life I found out her father was verbally abusive and used to compare my academic performance to hers. Not surprisingly, she was resentful and used the veiled put-downs to express her own frustration. As a young girl, I had no idea of what was going on in her world and could only feel that she was out to get me. Thankfully, knowing that I was well loved helped cushion her jabs. I am grateful to my parents for nurturing my very healthy self-esteem. Not only did this help me emerge from adolescence unscathed, but later I would rely on this strong sense of self-worth to persevere and not be defeated by circumstances that were beyond my control.

I am grateful to my parents for nurturing
my very healthy self-esteem.

By the time I was of college age, I was one of the few in my graduating class who was able to leave Venezuela to pursue a higher education. The choices within the country were mostly limited to private institutions in Caracas if one was serious about graduating and had the means to afford the tuition. Public universities were constantly on strike and it was not unusual for the pursuit of a degree to take 8 or more years.

Black Friday crushed such aspirations for a number of my friends and was life altering for many others. Notably, some families had weathered the economic storm but were uncomfortable with the notion of sending their daughters to study abroad. However, I was ready for the experience of going away and this was beyond the notion of academic advancement. Most of my peers were out clubbing and partying since they were 14 years old. Because the crime rate was steadily on the rise, my parents were very protective and limiting. As an adolescent this would have been stifling and most would rebel, but I was always reasonable because I recognized the dangers and could understand their concerns. Instead, I looked forward to my summers in Panama where I was unrestricted to come and go as I pleased with my cousins. We would zip around the city, checking in and out of parties till late at night. Having tasted the sweetness of unrestrained youth, I was excited to leave Venezuela to enjoy the permanent sense of freedom that a safe environment in another country would allow.

Reaching For the Stars

"And now these three remain: faith, hope and love.
But the greatest of these is love."

1 Corinthians 13:13

*A*s the notion of choosing a career loomed ahead, I was conflicted. I had been the only student to ace Art History, taught by a stern, demanding, but much beloved professor. All his instruction came alive the following summer at the Louvre when I could name the masterpieces and their backstories. In addition, the nuns allowed me to cut classes to paint murals and billboards around school. In the confines of a strict all-girls catholic institution, I thought it was cool to look the part of a bohemian artist, my uniform stained by pastel or tempera, as I roamed freely around the halls while everyone else was in class.

Clearly, I leaned towards the Arts, but I was also a high performer in Chemistry, Math and Physics. Mine was a double whammy: the Chinese legacy and the Latin reality. In those days, pursuing anything that was remotely artistic in Venezuela guaranteed a perpetual slot on the family payroll. Law, medicine or engineering were viewed as solid careers whereas the arts were ephemeral and unpredictable. Such endeavors were not encouraged by my father. When I tested with equal aptitude for interior design and engineering, his sage advice was "studying engineering is for the young, but the artist within you can be picked up at any stage in life." I think I would have made a pretty awesome interior decorator, but I heeded his counsel and decided to pursue a degree in Industrial and Systems Engineering.

**Studying engineering is
for the young, but the artist within you can be
picked up at any stage in life.**

Many times I've been asked, "Mexico? Why did you go to school there?" The answer was simple: I was a legacy student. Having visited his Alma Mater to ascertain it remained the caliber school that he remembered, my father was pleased with what he saw so I attended the Monterrey Institute of Technology in Mexico. Affectionately referred to as the "Tec" by its alumni, the main campus is located in Monterrey, Nuevo Leon. Monterrey (with two "R's") is a highly industrial city in the arid northern border of Mexico, known for its steel and cement production and not to be confused with Monterey, California which is considerably quainter, charming and right next to the ocean. My mother would have preferred an experience in the American educational system, which had eluded me. Because I was only sixteen years old when I graduated from high school, she agreed a conservative Latin environment would be unlikely to cause a culture shock and was the best option as my first foray away from home.

- "Why am I going to Mexico? I always thought I'd go to the States." I questioned.

- "We think going away to a Latin country will be easier for you. If you don't adapt, you can always transfer to the US in your second year" was their response.

I think we humans find comfort in facing the unknown when there is a contingency plan, an alternative to mitigate the finality of a decision. Even though I had never been to Mexico, I was happy to land in the uncharted because I knew there was another path if I did not like the Tec.

Like my dad, I was very young when I left home— I had yet to turn seventeen. Unlike him, I had ample experience with air travel as I flew back and forth from Venezuela to Panama for the summers. Although my whole family journeyed to drop me off at the onset of my first semester, it was up to me to navigate the subsequent travel at the end of each term. It was quite an exercise in logistics which gave me much perspective when I observe other parents fret about sending their kids away within the United States . . . the same country! My hometown, Valencia, was a two-hour drive away from Venezuela's international airport. There I would board a flight to Mexico City with a layover somewhere in Central America which was no big deal. Upon arrival, I had to negotiate immigration, customs and then take a second flight to Monterrey. Finally, I had to secure a ride to my dorm with friends because Mexican cab drivers were deemed unsafe for an unaccompanied young girl. Clearly, my parents were confident that I was ready to be off on my own just as much as I looked forward to relishing my independence and freedom.

I am forever grateful to them for funding my studies and their values beholding education as a major parental responsibility. Both my brother and I were offered the same opportunities, regardless of our gender. To this day, the Tec continues to be one of the premier educational institutions in Latin America and is ranked amongst the top 200 in the world. As an Industrial Engineer from this school, I was definitely employable, could start a savings account, and was on my way to becoming an exemplary corporate citizen. My training to observe inefficiencies, increase productivity and manage costs were cornerstone skills to my budding career. Little did I know how they would also serve me to advance my own family after our sudden loss.

Both my brother and I were offered the same opportunities, regardless of our gender.

As I was wrapping up my last semester at the Tec, I met the man I would marry in the most unusual and unlikely circumstances. Randy had just disembarked off the SS Universe, a ship that was home to a voyaging university program called Semester at Sea. Sponsored by the University of Pittsburg, it was a program offered to college students from all over the country to participate in a once of a lifetime experience. They would attend classes while at sea and then visit ports of cultural or human interest such as Egypt, Malaysia, Russia . . . In the naivete pre-9/11, about 1000 students at a time descended in the ports of these far-flung locations without a care in the world. They were there to immerse themselves in local cultures and expand their global perspectives.

Shared experiences can form strong bonds in a relatively short time. Randy became close with a fellow Mexican student who also happened to be my friend. When the Semester at Sea experience was over, Cesar, our mutual connection, concocted a spring break expedition for Randy to see "real" Mexico. I was invited to participate. The plan was for us to drive from Monterrey to Mexico City (12 hours away), meet up with Randy (who was flying in from California) and Victor (a fourth adventurer). After buying supplies and stocking up, we would head to Oaxaca ... all in a Volkswagen shift combi that served both as transportation and shelter. Such an adventure would be unthinkable today but in the late 80's we had no fears of danger, drug lords or bandits.

It was a tough trip. Adventure expedition was a mild description of our travels. Mostly we camped in sites "created" by hacking the grass off the side of the road with a machete or pitching a tent on the beach. Showers were non-existent. I felt and looked as equally gross as the rest of my fellow travelers. It was primitive at best, but my wish to see the Mexico of colorful markets, indigenous people, and the famous Doña Rosa pottery was being fulfilled. As a northern city, Monterrey was bustling and modern, but it lacked the cultural heritage of the great Pre-Colombian empires such as the Olmec, Aztecs or the Maya. None of my Mexican friends were particularly interested in going to the areas I wanted to explore. I suppose this would comparable to a college senior wanting to visit the indigenous culture of New Mexico for spring break. Who would want to go to Santa Fe over hot spots like Ft. Lauderdale, Daytona or in my case, Acapulco or Cancun? But my time in Mexico was nearly over, and I wanted to see more of this wonderful country that had been my home for the last 5 years. I wanted to see the authentic and folkloric Mexico.

We visited the archeological site of Monte Alban, the markets in Oaxaca, the lagoons of the Pacific and many other off the beaten path places of interest. On this trip Randy acquired a huge black clay pot housed in an even larger straw casket. Shipping this to California was a logistical challenge that did not dissuade him. I, instead, bought two equally beautiful pots that were much smaller and manageable. This rather obscure anecdote was a metaphor of our natures: The dreamer who made big things happen (him) and the pragmatic and sensible one (me).

Being the only fluent English speaker on the expedition, we ended up naturally pairing off for the driving, so we had ample hours to talk.

As we got to know each other, we realized that we had many thoughts in common. Speaking with the freedom of two airline passengers seated together, we chatted openly, thinking we would probably never cross paths again. He was unlike anyone I had ever met, with the coolness of a surfer, the eye of an artist, the savoir faire of a world traveler and the self-reliance of an outdoorsman. To Randy, life had no limits. He had the confidence that he could make everything possible and he approached each undertaking with boundless optimism and certainty.

Although he did not make a strong first impression on me, nor was I initially attracted to him, as we traveled together, I found myself enjoying his company and conversation. He was sensitive and open, a good listener and although we came from very different backgrounds, many of our thoughts aligned. Randy was impressed with my stamina because this trip was not for the faint of heart, nor the reliant on creature comforts. "I knew you were no girly girl when you willingly climbed into the van, burning from the midday sun, to rearrange our storage space. You had sweat beaded on your nose and dripping all over your face."

The turning point in our nascent relationship happened when the van's light broke down. While Cesar and Victor were busy fixing it, Randy and I had time to explore and roam the markets together. Later that day, when we finally arrived at a beautiful miniature bay that was to be our next camping site, we again ended up together snorkeling and playing in the warm waters. That night, as we lay on the sand gazing at the stars and enjoying each other's company, Randy kissed me. From that moment on, we were inseparable.

We explored the beaches looking for turtles in the moonlight, went horseback riding on the coast and thrived in each other's company. The natural beauty that surrounded us only served as a paradisiacal backdrop to nurture the feelings conceived on that moon lit bay. Even the most mundane camping chores like washing our cooking utensils, cleaning up the campgrounds or loading the van became likable because we did them together.

With limited opportunities to bathe, most of the trip we were all rather disgusting, looking more like unwashed hippies than the clean-cut college kids we really were. On the last night of our adventure, our group went out to dinner in Mexico City after a proper shower. As I descended the stairs of Cesar's home, wearing a long black dress, Randy's eyes almost popped out of his sockets when he saw me. "Wow, you are beautiful," he remarked before his natural reservation allowed him to hold back any comments. At that moment I knew that he had seen me first as a person and later, as an attractive young woman.

Along the way of this Mexican adventure, that free spirited photographer from California and this conservative Chinese Latina fell in love. Randy had been much more expressive with his feelings, telling me that night that he loved me and would come to visit me in Monterrey. I was much more cautious. The notion of never seeing Randy again was deeply unsettling, but I felt that the distance between us was too great to overcome. The practical and pragmatic side of me could not admit that I too had fallen in love.

**At that moment I knew that he had seen me first
as a person and later, as an attractive young woman.**

The following morning, we all drove to the airport to drop off Randy who was flying back to California. Right after Cesar and I would return to Monterrey. After helping unload his huge black clay pot, we said goodbye and parted quickly with a stolen kiss. Cesar was surprised because he had nothing but a mere hint of what had taken place between us. As we drove away, mired in sadness as never before in my life, I finally had the courage to recognize my feelings for Randy. I turned to Cesar and said:

- "I think I fell in love with your gringo friend."

Cesar's bushy eyebrows threatened to jump out of his forehead, and he cracked up realizing he had been blind-sided. Even though we were all cramped together during the expedition, he had been clueless. Over their four months on Semester at Sea, Randy had become his best friend. They shared many adventures in exotic locations, including a flat tire in Morocco where they tried to engage the locals for some help. "Ze tyre eezz flat," said one of them and then they both doubled over laughing. Speaking in English with a fake French accent was not going to get them anywhere. Far better were the universal gestures of mimicking a steering wheel and the hissing sounds of a deflated tire.

Cesar and I fell into a pensive silence as we drove the long hours to Monterrey. Finally voicing our thoughts, we concluded it was unlikely for something between Randy and I to ever materialize ... this was a romance with a doubtful future. In a few months I would finish my undergraduate studies and return to Venezuela, while Randy still had another two years of college ahead of him in California. Cesar knew that Randy had accepted a job in Alaska for the summer, so it was highly improbable he could visit me in Monterrey. However, I felt guilty of withholding my true feelings from Randy, thinking we had reached the end of what had just begun.

Penning my thoughts was the best I could do to soothe my uneasy conscience, so I rushed to write Randy a letter. Regardless if I ever saw him again, he deserved to know the depth of the emotions that I had for him. Meanwhile, Randy himself was going insane, missing me. Later he would reveal that I was present in every corner of his mind. He realized that he could visit me before going to Alaska, but would I want him to come? He expressed these feelings in a note card with a handful of roses that must have crossed my letter somewhere along the way. We both received our correspondence on the same day, one week after saying goodbye to each other.

Regardless if I ever saw him again, he deserved to know the depth of the emotions that I had for him.

Cesar fancied himself playing Cupid, so he let the cat out of the bag and told me that a package was on its way from Randy. It was agonizing to count the days for it to arrive and I was ecstatic with the contents. My response was immediate. Randy was merely a phone call away and he was waiting for my answer. Cesar also gave him a heads up about my feelings, so he had an inkling on what to expect. All he needed was to hear my voice to book his tickets. After a long conversation that seemed way too short and probably cost a small fortune, we made plans for him to fly to Monterrey.

The days leading up to his arrival went by ever so slowly and my emotions ranged from excitement to worrisome. What if we had been entrapped by the beauty of the nature that surrounded us? Was it merely infatuation? Were our feelings for real? Finally, the long-awaited day arrived, and I drove to the airport to pick him up. He was the most expected person coming off that plane and also the last one to clear customs. Randy had carried a bouquet of roses in his lap for the entire flight, so he walked out to greet me with flowers. Romance was apparent to all of the bystanders who viewed our reunion laced with excitement, roses, pleasure and nervousness.

The next few days were intense with many activities—it seemed we did not have enough time for ourselves. Pope John Paul II was visiting Mexico and Cesar planned another tiresome trip to Durango which was the closest location we could access (9 hours away). Waiting for hours to see His Holiness, we realized amidst the dust, heat and thirst, that every discomfort was tolerable if we were together. We both felt the same: amazed at finding one and other. It was like our souls had reunited after a fortuitous set of circumstances brokered our reunion. Our friends on each side of the border scoffed at the idea of a long-distance relationship. My posse had included some good looking and popular proverbial "bad boys" who were certain we were doomed to fail from the onset. My girlfriends were hopeful but doubtful. We forged ahead.

**It was like our souls had reunited after a
fortuitous set of circumstances brokered our reunion.**

Randy was the quintessential California beach boy: surfer, skier, dreamer, artist. He grew up in Huntington Beach, within walking distance to the ocean where he surfed on a near daily basis. Although he loved the water, he also enjoyed roaming around terra firm on his dirt bikes, motorcycles and cars. After winning a local motocross race, he decided that one trophy was sufficient for being on the edge and out of control. Not one to enjoy team sports, his real love was skiing which he did with Olympic caliber talent. Bystanders would line up to see him tear down the slopes in Mammoth when he was a young daredevil.

A jack of all trades, as a teen Randy owned a pool cleaning route bought by his father (probably to keep his sons busy and out of trouble). He also worked hanging wallpaper, painting cars, flipping burgers and had a myriad of other part-time jobs. His favorite was being a deckhand for Balboa Yacht Club in Newport Beach because he loved the ocean and being surrounded by the beauty of the boats and their sails. When the old dockmaster unexpectedly died, he took over the job since he was the most capable worker around. At 20 years of age, he suddenly was earning a 40K salary. Naturally, he dropped out of college. Randy was in charge of managing all of the comings and goings pertaining to the docks and tenders at the club—including keeping the members happy and content. This lasted for a couple of years. Upon realizing that customer service did not run in his blood, job security hinged on pleasing the members, and dockmaster positions were few and far in between, he decided to complete his higher education.

I fell in love with an explorer, sailor and outdoorsman who once considered a career in Forestry. The artist in him won out, always appreciating the natural beauty of our world: a sunset, the desert, a raindrop. After much research, he decided to pursue photography and enrolled at Brooks Institute in Santa Barbara, California. At that time, Brooks was one of the most prestigious photography schools in the world. He had found the perfect medium to express his poetry, capturing the world as he saw it, as how it ought to be. The dormant creative in me was enthralled and enchanted to see the world through his lenses and at his side.

My parents wanted me to pursue an MBA right after college, but I sought work experience prior to graduate school. After graduating from the Tec, I returned to Venezuela for the summer. Given all of my father's industry contacts, the logical next step was to find a job back in our hometown. However, I knew that our long-distance relationship could survive only if I returned to Mexico. Even though we were practically on opposite ends of North America with a border in between, this was logistically manageable. Venezuela was not.

At 21 years of age, I had never experienced a major life disappointment. With naive optimism, I confidently made one single long-distance phone call to the Dean of the Tec's Graduate Business Program. He was related to a close friend and I had spent many weekends at his home. Much to my parents' astonishment, in less than three days, Dr. Otalora secured me the perfect one-year job and I was set to return to Monterrey.

It was pretty amazing how two distant, different and diverse people came together. As I look back, I can only surmise that love that is meant to be will be—God will provide assistance to make dreams a reality and that our lives can be the product of a serendipitous moment. If Dr. Otalora did not have a relationship with this particular CEO or had he not bothered to make that call, Randy and I couldn't have pursued our relationship and my life as it has unfolded would not exist. I find it amazing how a single action can have such a ripple effect on another person's life. We might be forever ignorant of our impact on someone else's reality, but paying it forward has an entirely different meaning to me these days.

**...love that is meant to be will be–
God will provide assistance to make dreams a reality...**

Having the job in Monterrey allowed our romance to blossom, albeit still with distance as a major factor. Technically, Randy was still a student at Brooks in Santa Barbara. With the cleverness and drive that I would later observe in our sons, he translated the startup of his Mexican postcard company with Cesar to a "work-study." This earned him credits towards graduation while traveling to nurture our budding relationship. Three birds with one stone: school, girl, and a business.

In those days, every dime we earned went to pay our phone bills (one month it was $600) or for the airfare to see each other. In my first visit he was anxious to show me as much as possible, from meeting his family in Huntington Beach, to visiting his school in Santa Barbara, and going camping in the Sierras which he loved. My prior experiences, including that rough trip when we met in Mexico, stemmed from necessity rather than enjoyment. As a family we had visited the Venezuelan Grand Savannah, a remote area that bordered with Brazil where sleeping accommodations were nonexistent. Because it was so desolate, you had to bring your own supplies, including gasoline. Randy wanted to show me his version of enjoying the outdoors.

The first place I ever visited with him was Lone Pine in the California Sierras. The campgrounds seamlessly blended into the landscape and each site was well-equipped, groomed and managed. I was delighted to camp in a location that was undisturbed, pristine and yet civilized.

- "I'm off to go fishing," he announced.

- "Where are you going? Not that little stream next to our camp site?"

- "Yes, that one" he said confidently.

- "You are joking, aren't you?" I was incredulous.

Much to my astonishment he appeared a few minutes later with a fresh trout to fry. My prior experience was fending off Amazonian piranhas that

49

had to be clobbered as soon as they landed in the boat. Otherwise you risked being bitten and maimed by their powerful snapping jaws which could reduce a living cow to a skeleton in minutes. I never expected he would pull something edible out of the stream bordering the campground. Later, as we departed Lone Pine, I spied the stocking truck emptying trout into the stream . . . simply for the pleasure of the campers. I could not help but find contrast in this seemingly insignificant instance between the US and Latin America. It was the first time I appreciated the infrastructure that was implicit in the underpinnings of a first world country.

In tandem with working my first job out of college, I was also preparing to apply for Business School. At least that was "The Plan"— slightly delayed by my work detour. At this point, my parents did not quite take my American boyfriend seriously, so all was calm on the home front. He did visit Venezuela to spend Christmas with us (which should have been a major red flag) and we enjoyed the beaches and beautiful sites that were the setting of my childhood. That visit would turn out to be the last time I stayed in the house where I grew up and saw the country that was so generous to my family.

I appreciated the infrastructure that was implicit in the underpinnings of a first world country.

Applying to business school was a major undertaking: from taking the TOEFL, a test to verify that I could read and write in English, to the GMAT, a standardized test for graduate school. In addition, I had to write numerous essays and procure recommendation letters in an era where faxes were a new technology and such a thing as e-mail or even the internet was non-existent. All of that work paid off and I was accepted into several programs— both in Mexico and the US. I decided to go to Rice University, in Houston, Texas.

Upon wrapping up my one-year job in Monterrey, we moved to Houston. I would start my MBA and he would finish his undergraduate studies and work at one of the big city studios. For the first time the long-distance factor was removed from our relationship and we were able to experience the routine of being in the same city. Having normalcy led to his proposal a few weeks prior to my graduation. We announced it to both sets of parents when they came for the grandiose occasion.

It was heart wrenching that mine were deeply opposed. It was upsetting to him and devastating to me. Even though they had met Randy, my parents were surprised that our relationship was that serious. I had to wear dark glasses to my graduation ceremony to mask my swollen eyes from crying. There was palpable tension between our families. This was the first time they had met, and the circumstances could not have been worse. The Faris' were understandably dismayed and uncomprehending as to my parents' stand of opposition.

My parents were upset that I wanted to marry ... a free- spirited American photographer from California. Aside from the very real cultural differences, their concept of a photographer was he who snaps passport pictures. To them, this was not a career and they could not imagine how he would possibly provide for a family. In addition, Randy was quiet and reserved, a far departure to the Latin warmth and expansiveness that could have won them over. He was not a big personality and would rarely attract attention to himself. Instead, he found satisfaction through artistic expression or by simply "doing or being." Although they never said it out loud, their message to Randy was that I was "too good" for him. It was confusing and hurtful to him, but he never expressed any resentment towards them.

Up to that point, I had followed "The Plan" with admirable precision. They hoped that I'd eventually meet and marry a young man with a similar background and ethnicity. Quite frankly, that was seemingly impossible. I was 23 years old and had already lived in four countries and was a citizen of two. Although I was Panamanian by birth, I had spent my formative years in Venezuela and Mexico. I felt part of all three countries, but I could not single out any one of them as my motherland. I spoke in Spanish and dreamt in English. Even my own cousins could not relate to these circumstances.

Although I was 100% ethnically Chinese, we were not "FOB's" (that would be Fresh Off the Boat). We had already lost our ancestral language and many old-world customs. I was westernized, Latina and Catholic—yet there were cultural sensibilities from my eastern heritage that were still intrinsically woven into me. Today it is my privilege to be a naturalized US citizen but at the time, I simply considered myself a citizen of the world. This background is confusing to most, fascinating to some, and completely normal to me. I was happily "a cultural mutt."

I imagine that my parents considered my deviation from "The Plan" to be disconcerting at the very least. A major chasm opened which was deeply unsettling since they had always supported all of my decisions. Randy, through no fault of his own other than loving and wanting to marry me, was the object of my mother's derision. Although my father was not enthralled, thankfully he was able to mask his feelings. However, I was in the middle.

But ours was a love that was destined to conquer distance, culture and yes, even my family. I loved his gentleness, his thoughtfulness, and his quiet but unpredictable humor. Never one to attract any attention to himself, he would utter the most hilarious and insightful comments under his breath, just loud enough for one or two people to hear and burst out laughing hysterically. All who were close to him thought he was one of the funniest people they ever met. He had the habit of bringing humor to the most improbable of situations.

One time we were at some bar in the middle of nowhere in Mexico. It was more of a watering hole than a proper establishment. Straw covered the dirt floor and laborers arrived at the end of their day to drown their sorrows. We were conspicuously out of place—definitely an oddity in their midst—but everyone kept to themselves. With a mixture of shock and disbelief, we noticed that about ten feet away from us one of the corners had become an ad-hoc urinal. "Gene, five bucks if you give it a try," he muttered to my brother. We all burst out laughing. I think we laughed to cover our nervousness. As a mother of boys, I can only imagine his truancy in the classroom. I'm sure it was excused only because he excelled as a student.

He had the habit of bringing humor to the most improbable of situations.

Randy's parents were rightfully proud of their son and always supportive of his moves. His older siblings worked in the family business as accountants and they lived within miles of each other. He chose to do his own thing in a different direction. Always top of his class at Brooks, his talent was already garnering accolades and awards. He had just been selected to join a group of professional photojournalists—sponsored by Nikon and Kodak—to foster closer ties with the USSR. In all likelihood, they were the first and last westerners to visit remote locations of the former Soviet Union. Two weeks after that expedition, Boris Yeltsin won the election and declared Russia's independence. Upon graduation, Randy was singled out as a unique achiever from his generation. At commencement, he received a special award reserved for a handful of Brooks alumni who had been equally distinguished as young talents. Each of these recipients went on to become luminaries in their profession, including Randy.

To his credit, Randy encouraged my move to South Florida where I had accepted an offer from Baxter Healthcare, a Fortune 500 company. My parents had just made the momentous decision to leave the nascent turmoil brewing in Venezuela. They relocated to Florida, and I would be living with them. Again, we would be apart until Randy could make the move out of Houston. Now I would be within their sphere of influence as never before in our relationship. They still were not accepting of him and I was very conflicted about this whole morass. I was very close to them, but I loved and wanted to marry Randy. Professionally, it was an elating year. Personally, it was a debacle.

Deciding to marry Randy was my first departure from the protective cocoon of my parents' wisdom. My family danced to a tune named "Reasonable" and such was my default disposition, almost never deviating from their directives. Usually we aligned, which they might have interpreted as obedience. But to me, it was simply common sense or being smart. This was the first time I met their opposition in a decision of consequence, and I could not fully fathom the depths of their disapproval. All along, I believed I had passed the test of being an adult with flying colors, evidenced by being released at sixteen and subsequently navigating life with unquestionable excellence. Given our arduous discussions, I had given thought to the challenges that might lay ahead in an intercultural marriage. Nonetheless, I felt capable of making this next life choice on my own. I expected them to be supportive and I was disturbed because they were not.

I had no doubt that Randy cherished me. Just the fact that he patiently put up with my mother's attitude was evidence to me. Had the roles been reversed, I cannot say I would have reciprocated or been as gracious. His best friend, Duwayne was of Chinese and Japanese ancestry, so he could relate to some of the cultural idiosyncrasies. Even so, he'd remark, "Dude, why do you put up with their sh*t?" Despite the conflict, Randy was respectful of my parents and my relationship with them. I vacillated but was certain there was something special between us. I felt that we were meant to be together. Regarding his ability to make a living, I was confident of his talent. I knew he was a high achiever and I chose to disregard the fact that I was out-earning him.

For many months I prayed to the Lord for guidance because I was not getting what I needed from my family. Love prevails and faith sustains. I anchored my hope in our feelings and what we had overcome to be together. Finally, after five years of managing our long-distance relationship and jumping through high hoops, we married on June 10, 1995.

For many months I prayed to the Lord for guidance because I was not getting what I needed from my family. Love prevails and faith sustains.

"Deb is a junior executive" he would proudly say about me, loving that I was excelling in the corporate world. Back then, I thought my career was commonplace: the result of being a dedicated student, making sensible choices and always giving the best of my abilities to my employer. With age comes perspective. I now realize the uniqueness of these tightly packed and singular projects in my twenties.

As my first job in the United States, I landed in the international division of Baxter, an office populated by high chiefs and very few Indians (that would be me). Being perfectly bilingual with a clear understanding of the Hispanic culture afforded me a razor-sharp edge. Early on I was tasked with responsibilities that were beyond my qualifications simply because there was no one else within the office who could do the mid-level work. I relished the challenge while I was deeply aware that what I was doing would impact the livelihood of the workers and families at the manufacturing facilities. The data I gathered and analyzed was used for either growth or attrition decisions . . . one being exciting and the other emotionally depleting.

While not necessarily financially ambitious, I was driven to soar in my undertakings. Before, this drive manifested in my academics. Later, as an employee, it would show up in getting things done and executing seemingly impossible corporate mandates. With the confidence imbued by my parents and my education, I quickly rose through the ranks of Baxter's manufacturing world. Within a handful of years, I had logged over a million miles with American Airlines as I darted from one corner of the globe to another, evaluating multimillion-dollar investments, closing down manufacturing departments and moving the making of products across continents. My peers respected and admired me, my bosses were pleased with my performance, and I was in a great place career-wise.

My paycheck provided stability while Randy was on assignment traveling and shooting for Westlight, a stock agency. Nowadays, the internet provides free image content in digital form. Back then we were experiencing the last years of the film era, paper catalogs and entire staffs that collaborated with advertising agencies to supply photographs for a fee. Founded by acclaimed National Geographic photographers, Westlight was a commercial library with thousands of images that could replace the hiring of a professional photographer.

When the going gets tough, I remind my sons to align their wishes with God's purpose for them, that good can come out of any disappointment, and that it is pointless to wallow in self-pity. Obviously, hindsight and age proffer this wisdom, but I used their father's example to make it real. Prior to graduating, Randy had accumulated an impressive body of work from his travels around the world. He loved to photo journal the people, cultures, and natural beauty of the places he visited. He was aware of his technical abilities, but he also recognized his limitations when working with people. Sensitive and reserved, he did not have the personality to be on stage, to elicit emotions from his subjects, or the patience to handle their quirks. He was better suited to work on his own and hoped this student portfolio would pave the entry into a stock photography agency.

I remind my sons to align their wishes with God's purpose for them, that good can come out of any disappointment, and that it is pointless to wallow in self-pity.

After applying and being rejected by the two largest agencies, his best option was to accept the offer from a small company called Westlight. A contract with one of the corporate titans would have been more prestigious, but he would have been one of the many suppliers. Because of its size, Westlight's founder was very involved and ran the show. Consequently, he was spotted and mentored by one of the industry's visionaries. Craig Aurness recognized Randy's potential, invested in him and was a pivotal reason why my husband became one of the top stock photographers in the world.

With Craig's backing, Randy crisscrossed the US a number of times, capturing the main sights in all the cities he visited. In the early years of our marriage, he was on the road most of the time but then again, so was I. We managed to coincide a few times, most memorably meeting up in Australia. Baxter was sending me to Sydney for some meetings and Randy managed to finagle the budget to join me. The first half of the trip, we enjoyed first class accommodations provided by Baxter. After that, we found our lodging through The Lonely Planet traveler's guidebook, managing to stay at places a step up from youth hostels. Our adventures took us out to the Outback and to Uluru or Ayer's Rock. As I gazed at the incredibly clear night sky, I saw the Milky Way for the first time, with comets and falling stars dancing to a delicate celestial light show. The vast universe had probably fascinated my ancestors as they would have gazed upwards on many a cloudless night. As a modern human, I rarely looked up to the night skies with wonder because the city lights and every day distractions would opaque the celestial bodies. We no longer look up to the heavens because we can't see the stars.

Aside from traversing the US, Randy's assignments landed him in flung corners of the globe, including a memorable circuit through French Polynesia—from Tahiti to Bora Bora—where he cycled with a backpack. Despite all of his travels, Hawaii was his favorite location, with the added bonus that he could stay with Duwayne, who had moved to Honolulu. We spent our honeymoon in Maui and I was to visit this paradise on Earth a few more times before we became parents.

And so, I was happily and blissfully waiting at Miami International Airport as he returned from the 50th state. I was dressed in my billowing periwinkle muumuu, ready to nest and wait for this baby that was so much wanted and expected. After some rough months with severe morning sickness, my pregnancy was progressing beautifully. Everything had worked out. Life was normal, and our future as a young couple could not have seemed more predictably perfect.

Curveballs

"Therefore, what God has joined together,
let no one separate."

Mark 10:9

A few months after the baby's birth, we got battered by the first of many curveballs. Neither of us could have seen it coming. Had I been less ignorant, or had he been more aware, we probably would have known something was wrong. My inexperience and his denial delayed the inevitable. Upon Randy's return from Hawaii, I observed a newly acquired habit of drinking two or three beers at the end of the day. To this I remarked, "After the baby is born, the nightly beers are not a good idea." He agreed, and we did not give this another thought.

Alcoholism was the last thing on my radar because Randy rarely drank, only socially and then in very limited amounts. His favorite drink at a bar was a Tanqueray and Tonic which he'd nurse for the entire night if we went out. Otherwise, he would enjoy a beer or two if we grilled out socially. Alcohol was just not part of our dynamics. We had known each other eight-plus years and only once had I seen him slightly drunk.

In the era preceding our parenting days, we were with a group of friends preparing to spend a night on a deserted island off the Pacific coast of Panama. Although it might sound exotic and adventurous to the uninitiated, the prospect was anything but pleasant. Prior to falling asleep, Randy decided he needed some extra numbing to spare him from the reality of the tropical humidity and the annoying company of bugs and sand flies.

- "Deb, we should sleep on the boat with the captain, that's the best bunk in sight."

- "I'd rather be with the group. C'mon, don't be antisocial." Despite being a native, I was naïve about the experience we were about to have.

- "I'm not antisocial, but this is going to be rough. I'm gonna have to get drunk to get through this."

Rum and coke were his solution to the discomforts that lay ahead. With great humor, Randy proceeded to get sufficiently inebriated to ignore the tepid breeze and biting bugs. He was right: it was memorably awful. Nobody got a good night's sleep, and Randy was the only one who got through it mentally unscathed. This was the only time I had ever seen him somewhat intoxicated.

From our initial meeting until our first child, almost a decade had already passed. I had just turned 30 and was still making the most out of my ascending career. I imagined a baby would saddle me with new responsibilities and I was in no rush to take that next step until Randy reminded me that my biological clock was ticking. It was his idea to get started on trying to have a baby and we were shocked at how easily we conceived. I nested and enjoyed the many showers that co-workers, friends and family had planned for me while Randy busied himself making sure our house was ready. As part of his preparations, he managed his photo shoots so he could take a prolonged leave from work after the baby's birth.

His travel to Hawaii entailed many weeks away, but I was fine with his absence—except he was not around to alleviate the incredible hunger cravings that assaulted me during the first trimester. I was aware that he was meeting up every night with his bachelor friends, but such was our trust that I was happy and encouraging of his social time. Between both our travels, we were very independent, secure in the confidence that each other was true. One of the pillars in our marriage was absolute trust built upon the foundation of moving mountains and oceans to be together. When Randy went for a 6-week expedition to the Soviet Union, he was part of a large entourage of American and Russian photographers, travel officials and guides. As the group became cohesive after being in close company for a couple of weeks, he was shocked at the rampant promiscuity amongst the travelers, including the ones who had left spouses back at home. Because of the long-distance separation that we had already endured and had overcome, faithfulness was one of those values that neither of us ever questioned in our relationship.

One of the pillars in our marriage was absolute trust...

When the time to give birth approached, I was certain this would be the one time in my life to indulge in legit drugs. My mother was unwavering in her endorsement of the anesthesia. Growing up we rarely took aspirins, ibuprofen or any other form of medication. Her philosophy was to utilize natural remedies and to let the body heal on its own. Medicines were to be used only if all else failed. However, getting drugs to avoid the pain of childbirth was her one exception. "You say YES to that injection. There will be plenty of time in life to be a martyr, but childbirth is not one of them." Because our travel schedule conflicted with the regular classes, I hired a private Lamaze nurse for instruction. Upon reaching the breathing lessons, I flippantly told the nurse "Uhmm…You can skip through that section…I'm not gonna need to learn any of that because I'm getting my epidural."

My delivery was normal except for the delayed epidural since they needed to re-do some blood tests. Even though it was only two-hours, the pain I experienced was enough to send me over the edge. Randy was alarmed because he knew how much I was depending on that shot. I could endure discomforts or mental anguish, but I'm such a wimp for physical pain. Somehow, he managed to urge the nurses to hurry along the situation. I honestly don't know how women used to give birth without anesthesia.

Our first child enchanted me, and we bonded instantly. "Baby Faris" remained unnamed until a few hours prior to discharge because we could not agree on anything. I wanted a name that could be pronounced in both English and Spanish and none of Randy's suggestions sounded right. As I stared into his perfect little face framed by a full head of dark hair, it came to me as clear as a bell: "What about David?" I asked Randy. And so, our firstborn was to be named David, like the king he was in our lives.

Over the next few months, we both adapted to our new role as parents. I confess that it was trying. Parenting brought forth our innate traits as we tried to cope with the huge changes upon us. Being a classic type A, my approach was to learn and attempt to control the outcome. Meanwhile, Randy's "go with the flow" disposition was not helpful to me. Neither did I appreciate his soothing himself with a nightly beer or two. Rather than align, it seemed that we engaged in the Clash of Titans: control vs. addiction. This was when we started to diverge as a couple. As very independent opposites, his dynamic wanderlust and my stable practicality were often in conflict. I just could not be a free spirit when mothering an infant. The multiple feeding times, naps, and predictable diaper changes were boxing life into a routine I could handle but it was stifling to Randy.

Rather than align, it seemed that we engaged in the Clash of Titans: control vs. addiction.

After a four-month maternity leave, I returned to work. Three days later, Randy woke me up at the crack of dawn. "Deb, something is very wrong. We need to go to the hospital. I've been sipping beer for the last 36 hours and I can't stop." He was not inebriated or even buzzed. "If I don't have a can every couple of hours, I feel like I'm going to jump out of my skin." The guest room where he was sleeping was littered with empty cans. It was a sight I could not even begin to process as we rushed out of the house. Such was my alarm about going to the ER that my hands were trembling as I drove to the same hospital where I had given birth 4 months earlier. They detoxed him with Ativan. Upon discharge, no one offered an explanation to this situation except for the case worker mentioning he "might have a problem with alcohol." Nothing else was said and no further actions were prescribed.

To someone like me whose default mode is "cause and effect," this incident was upending to say the very least. What does "a problem with alcohol" mean? How did he end up having to be "detoxed"? This was a new word in my vocabulary. I had never heard it or used it in a sentence before. My research yielded vague answers, nothing definitive. I assumed that going to an ER would have struck Randy like a lightning bolt and that his reaction would have been the same as mine—to get to the bottom of this issue so it never happens again. However, he brushed it off as if it was a speck of lint on his shoulder and did not give it a second thought. This should have been a huge red flag to me, but at the time, I did not process his inaction as denial.

David did not sleep through the night until he was about 4 months old and he was invariably awake at the crack of dawn. I am one of those people who need a full 8 hours to function, so sleep deprivation became a keen issue for me. My temper became short and any patience I had was reserved for the baby—there was nothing left for my husband. I had no idea how disruptive this new life stage was going to be. "You've become the sleep Nazi" said Randy more than once because my life was starting to revolve around getting enough sleep to face the following day. Despite the warnings at my various baby showers, no one really prepared me for the intensity and the challenges of motherhood. Since I was breastfeeding, Randy could not help much with our new baby. To confront our new dynamics, he chose to find his "serenity in a can." As he indulged in his one or two end-of-the-day beers, I began to observe a shift in his nature.

**...no one really prepared me for
the intensity and the challenges of motherhood.**

He was less thoughtful, less considerate and less engaged with me. Having a beer when he wanted it was more important than my feelings. Likewise, I also started to change. The twenty-some year old that he had met was easygoing, nonchalant, and always game for an adventure. When David was still crawling, I remarked how much my life had shifted and his response was, "Nothing at all has changed for me." That he could not appreciate what I was juggling was stunning and revealing. No wonder I could not afford to be carefree. I had no emotional support from my spouse.

In retrospect, drinking a couple of beers daily (which was nothing to most) was not the problem. It was his behavior that troubled me. I could not comprehend how this man who had moved oceans and mountains for us to be together was not evolving with me as we assumed our new roles as parents. Randy had advocated for a baby before I even considered entering the theater of motherhood. We were often at odds, so I blamed the beers which had become my enemy. Being a planner was a positive trait that had served me well thus far, but that began to morph into a controlling wife who limited when, where and how much he could drink. It was not a becoming transformation. I was turning into a shrew.

As I began to read about alcoholism, I found that Randy was not checking any of the usual boxes. He was not blacking out, choosing beer over work, isolating himself or having extreme mood swings. He would say he needed to relax but who could blame him? The changes in his behavior towards me and our eroding relationship were the only red flags, but it was not unusual for marriages to shift upon the arrival of children.

Nonetheless, I simply could not attribute the tectonic shift in his personality to becoming a new dad. It had to be the drinking. But how could this be he was having only a couple of beers at the end of the day? My evaluation of "a problem with alcohol" was based on Randy's level of consumption, which was nothing out of the ordinary to most people. It was beyond bizarre and hugely conflicting. I was completely ignorant about alcoholism. Nothing in my past had ever brushed against the stain of this problem. My notions of an alcoholic were those of a lowlife who begs by the corner store, or the drunk who is inappropriate at the company party—but not the upstanding and capable man who was my husband. My parents were not drinkers and while I had seen my fair share in college, I was unfamiliar with the behavior of an alcoholic, not realizing that the negative consequences of substance abuse are much stronger signals than the actual consumption of the substance.

Randy was in denial there was even a problem. "C'mon Deb. What is wrong with a couple of beers at the end of the day?" Compared to the rum, whiskey, and tequila drinkers that I knew from my years in Venezuela and Mexico, his consumption was trivial. "I don't know. It just does not seem right, and it bothers me."

In the absence of "evidence" in the form of hard alcohol or copious beer guzzling, at times I entertained the notion that nothing was wrong, second guessing myself. I started to believe his accusations that all our problems were entirely my fault. "Motherhood is overwhelming you and you've become mean and impatient." Such were the inconsistencies between the information that was available to me at that time, the lack of stereotypical drinking, and the actual behavior that I was witnessing. I had no certainty of what I was facing. When I would consult with my friends or family, I was often at odds trying to explain what was going wrong, especially because there were long periods of abstinence and when he drank, it was only a couple of beers.

However, there was one situation that confirmed my suspicions. In the phase when I controlled his drinking, I "allowed" him to celebrate my cousin's graduation. It's laughable to think that I could police his drinking and that he would not resent my meddling, but this was the reality we were living in those days. Notably after only one glass of wine,

Randy reeked as if he were plastered when previously this was never the case. "Oh my goodness, how much did you drink tonight?" I asked as his breath and body exuded the fumes of booze. "Only one glass, when we made the toast." Somehow his body had changed so that he no longer processed alcohol as he had in the past. Instead, ingesting just a fraction was enough to make him stink. It was as if a switch had been flipped on. After this incident, I became increasingly certain that Randy was an alcoholic, a label that no one wanted to acknowledge, including myself. In any case, our relationship was going from bad to worse.

**Somehow his body had changed so that
he no longer processed alcohol as he had in the past.**

The love we felt for our first baby mitigated the downward spiral of our marriage. David was an active and delightful little boy who talked and walked before he was one year old. He was the light of our lives and the center of our attention. Every moment with him was sheer joy and I was astounded at being able to feel so much love for such a tiny being. Randy was also enchanted with his son and as David entered toddlerhood, he was able to participate more as a father.

Nevertheless, as the time passed our relationship was becoming marred by the cycle of my control, his denial, a period of abstinence, the eruption of a crisis, and the fight that would ensue. Every time this cycle repeated itself, the fractures got deeper as he denied, and I realized the truth of what was happening. My feelings for him shriveled and I must have been equally unattractive. At the time I was unaware that "pretending it's all right" was very much a coping mechanism in Randy's family. This lack of acknowledgement or "not taking the bull by the horns" left open the chasm for the next unsuspecting generation to fall in.

Alcoholism and anxiety ran through his paternal line. His grandfather and uncle were both drinkers and committed suicide, but this had been rarely discussed, and Randy was barely aware. His father had his own struggles with alcoholism over the years, a fact that was not acknowledged by Randy or his siblings. As an adult, Randy himself was in disbelief about his dad until it was inevitable. Conversely, he could not accept the legacy of alcoholism. Pathetically, I would remark that Randy must be Egyptian because he lived in the land of "De-Nile".

Because he was not the stereotypical alcoholic, it took me a long while to accept our own reality. I was indeed married to an alcoholic. It's a condition that is both physiological and psychological. For Randy, a quantity deemed insignificant to most was enough to make his personality change. It was not a matter of how much, it was a matter of what drinking did to his temperament. Conversely, the less he heard, the more I talked. If my normal default was being focused and attentive, I became fierce and intense. My worst character traits started to emerge— sarcasm and incessant nagging wrapped around the discordant harmony of an unhappy woman. Anger and fear peppered our eroding marriage like a sprinkling of gunpowder, ready to ignite with the smallest spark. I was simply over the top controlling, so all was my fault. Conversely, he was just drinking to sleep or handle the stresses of the day.

**It was not a matter of how much,
it was a matter of what drinking
did to his temperament.**

I sought help from our church, and we scheduled our first counseling session. Randy agreed to come but after the first meeting, he dropped out.

- "Can you help me? Can you help us?" I asked our counselor.

- "If he does not want to come, you will need to leave him."

This was so contrary to the solution I was expecting from a Catholic Deacon. I was aghast, but in hindsight, he was right. I should have presented that ultimatum much earlier on because perhaps, this would have opened Randy's eyes. Hope, fear, love, a slew of emotions kept me trapped and wrapped in unhappiness during my first year as a mother.

"Oh my goodness, we are like rabbits, are you kidding me?" Somewhere along the way, in trying to re-boot our relationship, I unexpectedly got pregnant with our second child. Meanwhile, our marriage was getting progressively worse. That second pregnancy gave me the levity to not take any major steps until after the baby's birth. I knew my emotions were all over the map. I was distressed, exhausted and in a state of despair with not much fight left in me. I did not want to make any major decisions until I regained some level of emotional stability and my capabilities (not to mention my hormones) returned to pre-baby days.

Under these circumstances, it is absurd to think that we were also house hunting. Being from coastal California, where real estate savior faire is elevated to the extreme, Randy had the eye to move us to a home that was located on a dream street: a double cul-de-sac in a great school district and on the water with ocean access. We purchased our home just in time to avoid the bubble that was starting to swell in Florida's real estate market. Deep inside I knew that if things did not change, I was going to leave but I played along—partly because I was hopeful and partly because I wanted to avoid further conflict.

During all of this time, my parents would come to stay with us for extended periods—at times two or three months. Their presence added much help in caring for David and an equal amount of tension as they witnessed our deteriorating relationship. I thought they would bond with Randy over their first grandchild, but that never happened. They could only see the deficiencies in his parenting or his lack of support towards me. My father, in his concern, also attempted to intervene with Randy so that he would acknowledge the problems that his drinking was causing and masking. He would say, "Usually a marriage is stressed because of at least one of these three reasons: money, cheating or substance abuse. You both are doing well. Deb would not cheat on you so what else is causing these problems?" The conversation was to no avail and again, I was in the middle, but now Randy was isolated and feeling like a stranger in his own house. I had once hoped that the baby would heal the rift, but the alcoholism was a wedge that had inserted itself into my aspirations and drove everyone farther apart.

I gave birth to Michael 23 months after David was born. Almost Irish twins. Considering the raging conflict that battled within and outside of me, this baby was incredibly placid and happy. Never upset and always smiling. Somehow, I had spared him from the angst I felt during the months between his conception and birth. It was as if I had sequestered all my positive feelings and everything that was good inside my womb and shielded him from the anger, anxiety and unhappiness that permeated the rest of my body.

Few can recall how they were parented before the age of five, but these memories are stored in our subconscious. I have been told that we emulate the care we received as infants when we are parenting our own children. This might explain the huge divergence between his and my style. My parents were very intentional with our upbringing. As an educator, my mother was incredibly conscientious about our emotional and mental development, resulting in a very nurturing environment as my brother and I were growing up. She was also very limiting about external influences, so the TV was never on at home until we were about 9 or 10 years old.

My child rearing philosophies were not in alignment with Randy's. At a time when we should have been coming together over our own children, we were instead growing apart. The drinking exacerbated our distancing. Somewhere along the way, the alcoholism awoke the dormant tigress that lived within me. I was fiercely protecting my cubs and their environment. Randy was not the man I had married, and I was evolving into a person I did not want to be.

The drinking exacerbated our distancing.

A month after Michael's birth we moved into our new house and a few weeks later I announced to him: "I want a divorce and I'm telling my mom and dad. You should tell yours." I had held out until the waters were calm before dropping my bomb. I had never threatened with the big D, but telling my parents meant that I was dead-serious and he knew it.

Within days, Randy found his own counselor and wanted us to give it another shot. I was reluctant but, in all fairness, I had to be open since he had at least agreed to try my Catholic Deacon. Even though my mother had never warmed up to Randy, they were both encouraging and hopeful. I grudgingly went to counseling with a less than skeptical attitude, but I had nothing to lose.

71

Much to my surprise, I found myself thinking that Susan could actually help us whereas all of my attempts to knock some sense into him had failed. We began to schedule weekly counseling sessions. She had already worked with a few photographers and understood the creative mind. Susan was direct and to the point with me, but she coddled Randy and lightly flitted around his issues. "Why do you pussyfoot around Randy's problems? He's the one that is wrong, I'm just reacting to everything he has created." I asked with more than a trifle of irritation. "Because you can handle the facts, but he needs to feel them to change. He will only hear me if I speak gently and softly." At that point, I seriously wanted to clobber my husband but instead deferred to Susan's wisdom.

She helped us grow up and get past this very rough patch in our marriage. With her we learned about nutrition, blood sugar issues and their correlation to alcoholism. She advocated alternative healing therapies including acupuncture and herbal remedies. Despite my ancestry, this was a new approach, but I was willing to embrace anything that was homeopathic or natural. Susan and I were on the same page, Randy was skeptical but had to go along with her suggestions since finding her was his idea. As he started to accept and work on his alcoholism, I began to loosen the reins and tone down the tiger mom behavior. Instead of being reactive, impatient and curt, I tried to relax and let go. For the first time in a long while, hope glimmered over our horizon.

Juggling two small children and my career at Baxter was not easy but with the help of a live-in nanny, I was managing to "do it all." At this point, I was less interested in climbing the corporate ladder than keeping an ace up my sleeve in case our marriage did not work out. Like never before was I was grateful for the backbone that my education and career were providing, confident of my ability to provide if we divorced. My job was leverage for him to continue working on his issues.

72

Because of 9/11 my early motherhood years became easier. This was disturbing but true. Prior to the attack, my work travel was usually unplanned and unforeseen which was a challenge with young children. Randy himself was traveling even more which was of no help either. In the aftermath of this terrible tragedy, jumping from country to country became more restricted and we learned to teleconference and communicate more effectively. I started working out of our home to maximize my time before the notion of telecommuting became popular in Corporate America.

**I was grateful for the backbone that
my education and career were providing,
confident of my ability to provide if we divorced.**

After four months of redirecting my office phone to our house, I called my boss (who was based out of Puerto Rico) and asked, "Carlos, have you noticed any difference with my work or my results?" He said he had not. "Well, I've been working from home all of this time." There was a moment of silence and then he replied: "Do whatever works best for you. Just don't make a big deal about it and don't tell anyone." Mornings were for Europe, followed by Latin America, a mid-day break to get out of my PJ's and take care of the domestic issues. More calls until the dinner break and maybe catch an episode of Desperate Housewives (to whom I related in more than a few ways). Usually I would wrap-up at midnight after a teleconference call with the Philippines, China or Australia. It was a crazy work schedule because there was no schedule at all, but the tradeoff was worthwhile: I was at home with my sons.

Once in a while, I'd still have to impromptu travel to the countries and leave the toddlers and their nanny all organized. It was exhausting to arrange meals for a week in advance while also prepare to leave at the drop of a hat. I was THAT career woman who pumped and dumped the liquid gold that is breast milk . . . in the tight confines of an airplane bathroom. It was disgusting, bizarre and incredulous—the life of the working modern mother.

While I was on one of these trips, the nanny told me (and I confirmed) that Randy was drinking while on daddy duty. I was first disappointed, then livid and ready to divorce again. I had let my guard down and I felt like I had been punched in my stomach. All the air was sucked out of me and a disembodied feeling overtook me as I processed her description of the home situation.

**I had let my guard down and
I felt like I had been punched in my stomach.**

Normally I would fall asleep on the 10-hour night flight from Sao Paulo to Miami. Much to the astonishment and envy of my fellow business travelers, I had mastered the art of getting a full 8 hours of rest—while up in the air. More than once, my seating companion would remark, "How in the world do you fall asleep and stay asleep for the duration of the flight?" For the first time though, I could not relax because the thoughts ruminated through my head incessantly. I was not worried about David and Michael's safety because their nanny was capable and responsible, but I could not understand why Randy would slip while I was gone. Did he depend on me that much to keep him accountable?

Randy was supposed to stop drinking and his flagrant disregard of being THE ONLY parent in charge incensed me at first and then it was downright deflating. I inventoried all of the implications of his drinking: he loves the booze more than me or the kids; he has no control; this will never go away. All of these thoughts converged and collided with the principal one: I just want everything to be all right and normal for our family.

Normal. What is normal? Honestly, at this point all I wanted was for nothing bad to happen. Randy had accepted his alcoholism and had pledged to remedy our relationship. I was alight with hope and then devastated to know that he had stopped trying, that he had reneged on his commitment to me, to us. I was incredibly deflated and disappointed, sinking to an even lower low. All the defenses that I had erected while on the path of emotionally extricating myself from this mess (i.e. divorce) got harder and harder to rebuild each time he faltered on the slippery slope of recovery.

Although I was certain Randy loved his sons, I was clearly the most present and responsible parent. Therefore, I was frightened by the idea that he would assert any custody claims over the boys. How would I ever know if he was sober and capable when he was in charge of David and Michael? Just the thought of what could happen gripped me with anxiety. Moreover, I was the main earner in the family and I had funded all our savings, so I should be entitled to the lion's share of our assets. I was certain to be the principal and possibly the only caregiver, so I needed financial peace of mind. In short, I wanted to avoid a custody battle or a fight over money.

Up in the air, with hours to think, I had the time to make a plan that would keep him accountable. It was straightforward, and in my opinion, brilliant. My premise was, "If you are really sincere about dealing with your alcoholism, then I am equally committed to us staying together." We wanted to preserve our marriage and the only thing that was messing this up was the drinking which was supposed to STOP. According to the prevailing AA wisdom, this is the commitment that even a one beer drinker or once a year binger must honor. If it's a problem, get rid of it—regardless of how small or infrequent. "IF you truly intend to stop drinking then all of our problems would go away and therefore, I will not proceed with a divorce."

If it's a problem, get rid of it–regardless of how small or infrequent.

Having this clarity, I delivered my next ultimatum: "Sign a Post-Nuptial guaranteeing that I'll get primary custody of the boys and entitlement to most of our assets. The terms of this document come into effect only if we enter divorce proceedings which in turn, will only happen if you can't manage your alcoholism." So simple.

To me, marriage was never supposed to be a transaction, it was a sacrament. We shared a great love and we had undertaken many personal sacrifices to make it a reality. I had overcome my family while he structured his career and moved away from his beloved California. As practicing Catholics, divorce was off the table until the intrusion of alcoholism reared its ugly head … a deal breaker. I just could not envision a future for us suffused in the fumes of the spirits. Just the thought and smell nauseated me.

Despite his very real desire to fix our marriage, this derailment was of consequence. Just when I had started to feel like there was hope, he had shattered that illusion and I was back to the drawing board. Such was my anger that I could not even remember what it felt like to love him. Our marriage had evolved into an agreement that was just not working out. I was so fed up that I was willing to entertain a transactional contract to protect myself and our children. In my head our marriage was no longer "us"— it was the kids and me.

At first, Randy balked at the idea because it was so lopsided in my favor. I stuck to my guns and remained adamantly stubborn. Truth be told, I had a patchwork of emotions going on: fear of an ending, hope for a solution, anger of being let down, sadness for my predicament, disbelief that this was happening to me, denial wanting to pretend all was right. I clung to the anger because it gave me the strength I needed to remain firm. I HAD to be determined: "If you want us to remain married, this is the only option that will give me peace of mind." Returning back to square one was emotionally depleting and I wanted my "get out of jail" card. "This gives me a pass on the custody battle or any of the nightmares of going down the path of divorce. You have to trust me just as much as I am relying on you." Embodying the dragon queen worked, and he capitulated to my demands.

**I clung to the anger because it gave me
the strength I needed to remain firm.**

I secured a lawyer who had a hard time understanding what I wanted. "A Post-Nuptial? Is that what you want? I don't understand." I had to explain "This is not a divorce. I need something that spares me from fighting just in case we go down that path." What I wanted was really an insurance plan, driven by a mixture of fear and in its own way, love.

I did not look forward to raising two little boys alone and I wanted my husband's support. He in turn needed my commitment to stay married so he could work on his addiction, putting the fear of abandonment aside. As weird as it may seem, this was our version of how to make our marriage work and to show our love to each other. Six weeks later, much to his credit because he had everything to lose, Randy signed the Post-Nuptial. This asymmetrical deal left him vulnerable and financially exposed, but he was relying on my values and character to not turn this around and betray his trust.

With this Post-Nuptial, I had achieved some semblance of stability. Once more, I began to relinquish control of his actions and focus my energies on raising our children. He had my full buy-in to support his recovery without the fears I associated with the "what ifs" should this not work out. This gave me a veil of security while we worked through all of our issues and he was truly accountable to his word. Somehow, we both gave each other the gift of commitment, and again, we lit the flame of hope in our marriage.

Glass Castles

"Above all, love each other deeply,
because love covers over a multitude of sins."

1 Peter 4:8

*I*t took work, time and money, but we were both committed and our marriage steadily improved. Finally, arduously, and with determination, we arrived at a junction where our styles were aligned and our vision on raising the boys was cohesive. After months of counseling, I was happy to freely divulge all I had learned, "This cost us about five grand; my advice is free to you." This is what I'd quip to friends in distress as I tried to make light and put that horrid episode of our life behind us. The silver-lining was that Randy's career started to take off into the stratosphere.

In the mid 90's, Bill Gates purchased the Bettmann Archives: a collection of carefully curated historical images dating from the inception of "the visual age." I suppose Gates' intention was to monopolize the image content of the world . . . but this acquisition was not a commercial success. The Bettmann photos were mostly destined for editorials or textbooks, the type of usage that collects minimum royalties. The lucrative side of stock photography was in commercial advertisement.

Hence, the beginning of this millennium saw the voracious consolidation of commercial photo libraries. Two major global players emerged from this buying spree: Getty (of the Getty family) and Corbis (owned by Bill Gates). When Westlight was acquired, Randy was the main photographer. This preeminence paved his transition into becoming a top content producer for Corbis in an era of deep pockets to fund advertising shoots. He had climbed to the apex of his career pyramid and was poised to soar.

All of a sudden, the budgets to lease stadiums, opera houses or iconic locations were generously available. Before Corbis, our friends, our kids and even I used to model for his photos, but now he could hire professionals without thinking about the cost. Sets and props went from simple to extravagant. His team could afford to lease F1 race cars at Silverstone in England, when before we used to make our own props. A production crew would assemble in Whistler, Buenos Aires or Prague to shoot images for the upcoming Winter Olympics, Soccer World Cup or the latest advertising trends.

This was a heady time for us. We were in our young thirties and were both bringing in six figure incomes with his significantly surpassing my salary. The supermodels of the era could be quoted saying, "I don't get out of bed for less than 10 grand a day." Randy and I used to laugh as he remarked, "Neither do I." Suddenly he was leaving behind his Motel 6 lodging, upgrading to 5-star hotels. He also found humor in the ludicrousness of riding the elevators with the "suits" while he was wearing cargo shorts and flip flops. He relished not having to dress up for work and that his wardrobe included bright ski jackets or cool wet suits to shoot in the snow or the ocean. Beneath all of this amusement rested the quiet pride of proving that he was making a significant living for his family. Even so, he was always respectful to my parents despite their early misgivings about his ability to be financially successful.

On Randy's shoulders rested the outcome of these funded shoots and he delivered beautifully. He teamed up with Pete, an old colleague from the Westlight era. Pete could produce, art direct, and work with the models while Randy concentrated on the technical issues. It was a flourishing partnership because Peter had the patience and soft touch to work with people which was Randy's shortcoming. When I modeled for him, I'd complain, "I'm not a prop. Stop twisting my head in such a weird way." Randy could only relate to the camera angle. Sometimes the poses were very unnatural, and he'd get exasperated that I could not comprehend what he wanted to achieve. Art direction and communication was simply not his forte. Instead, his innate visual talent was enhanced by having the skill to light any situation and his ability to deliver a large quantity of high-quality images. Some photographers would require a whole day to craft one image while Randy could produce 30-40 in the same time frame. His training at Brooks gave him the technical know-how. When combined with his artistry, it made him one of the top stock photographers in the world as recognized by his peers. He was not famous, but his work appeared in every single commercial medium imaginable. From billboards to movie posters, TV ads to magazine covers, even junk mail—and we received royalties from each usage.

He was not famous, but his work appeared in every single commercial medium imaginable.

A second home by the beach in California, a beautiful Grand Banks moored at Balboa Yacht Club in Newport, a Porsche and other toys followed. "Are you sure we can afford all of this?" Given my upbringing, I did not necessarily agree with all his purchases and was appalled at the expenses. "Yes Deb, you are a rich girl...live like one!" But I always reminded him, "We need to put some money away for retirement and not spend it all." I tried to establish a very sound savings philosophy for ourselves. Witnessing the capital flight that my parents were able to accomplish in Venezuela was a lesson that boomeranged back to me as an adult. Depending on our individual workload, both of us oversaw our investments and were equally competent in managing them. It was a blessing that I was so familiar with our banking because after he passed, the handling of our finances was a seamless transition instead of another traumatic learning curve.

**I tried to establish a very sound
savings philosophy for ourselves.**

During that same period, it was fitting for me to leave behind my corporate America days and fully delve into motherhood while also supporting our family business. My job had served its purpose as leverage and we no longer needed my income. I was somewhat tempted to climb the next step on the ladder: an ex-pat assignment in China. This was appealing because Randy was shooting frequently in Beijing and Shanghai. He was uniquely impressed with the latter, saying, "All that is missing are the spaceships" because it was such a modern and surreal city. I would have loved for our sons to learn Mandarin as their third language. My negotiations came to an abrupt halt when the SARS epidemic broke out and instead, I became Randy's assistant. It was definitely a downgrade with no pay, but I was more than ready to cease my executive life.

Except for the adjustment of working together, our marriage was finally stable, and we were happily normal. In the beginning we would have huge disagreements about my non-existent administrative skills. "I thought you were super smart" he'd remark when I'd forget to order toner or envelopes." Then I'd retort, "I do the big thinking. My assistant used to manage these things." When our arguments got heated (I was just not good at the minutia), he'd say, "Deb, if you were my employee, I'd fire you." To which I'd counter, "If you were my boss, I'd quit".

However, my project management skills in leading global initiatives easily translated into producing photo shoots, location scouting, finding props and hiring models. Finally, I was diving into the artistic world that had always fascinated me. His photography became even more significantly embedded into our life. We always brainstormed ideas together, enjoyed shopping or creating props and sets that would visually convey our concepts. Life was a lot of fun and everything—including our travels— was done equally for work and for pleasure. He was living his dream of doing what he loved, with whom he loved and being the best in his craft.

Our first photoshoot together was set in Hong Kong. Having grown accustomed to running the show on my business trips with Baxter, it was a mental adjustment to embrace the role of Randy's assistant. Far from the status of opening up global conferences, I was schlepping equipment, guarding location spots or helping the models with their wardrobe and make-up. It was enlightening to dive into his world and downplay who I was with the crew (few knew that I was Randy's wife). I was truly investing sweat equity in our business because Honk Kong is humid and hot. At the end of our trip, while Randy was in the hotel editing with Pete, I roamed the streets and spotted a beautiful sapphire and diamond ring in a nearby jewelry shop. "Deb, buy it. You deserve it after working so hard." This ring meant more to me than any bonus I received from Corporate America.

Randy's funded photo shoots usually meant a minimum of two weeks of travel each time he was on assignment, so I became used to managing everything on my own. If he was not away, he was readily available to help out with the boys and household. If I complained about the absences, he would remind me, "Few fathers are able to spend as much time with their kids as I do." He was right. We would summer in California and he would take about ten weeks off to be with our sons, mooring on Catalina Island or camping at Lone Pine. David, who was very attached to his father, was very mature for his age and mechanically inclined. Randy encouraged his innate curiosity by giving him old photo lenses to take apart or by working together building a tree house or wooden structures. They shared a unique father-son bond. David was the happiest when he was with Randy and his incessant conversation earned him the nickname, "Chatterbox."

Randy enjoyed translating his visual rendering of the world into experiences for the boys. Having grown up a short distance from Disneyland, he conceptualized his sets and props as what he had observed in this iconic park. One summer while shopping in San Francisco, we found some Spanish coin replicas of the gold that the buccaneers transported from the Americas to Europe. Later, while we were moored at White's Cove in Catalina Island, I created a pirate map and Randy hid the coins in a cave high up on a rock mound. He proceeded to entertain David and Michael with tales of pirates and booty as they "found" a bottle on the beach with a map that led them to the treasure. It was hard to know who was more excited— the children or their dad.

We had always intended for the boys to attend the Catholic school at our parish, but they did not have a program for three year-old children, so the staff at St. Joan referred us to St. Paul Lutheran. Once I noted the small class sizes, the loving warmth of the pre-school teachers, and their excellent academic reputation, we never left. There, the boys were thriving, and we were developing wonderful friendships along the way.

**Once I noted the small class sizes,
the loving warmth of the pre-school teachers, and their
excellent academic reputation, we never left.**

As the boys got older and entered pre-kindergarten and first grade, I looked forward to being involved in their scholastic activities. After being a room mom and helping out with a fundraising committee, I was recruited to join the PTA. In that role, I began managing some major fundraisers and the cadre of volunteers needed to make them successful, all of which was more in line with my project management background.

In retrospect, I suppose those loving catholic nuns might have cemented the foundations of my fundraising abilities. When I was about 12 years old, I delighted the Sisters with a bag full of coins and bills I had gathered to support their mission to the poor. They did not intend for me to overhear them when I delivered my stash. 1 "Look at how much this little one raised. She collected the most!" Although I was not aiming to compete with my classmates, I felt inordinately pleased to have impressed the nuns. Likewise, my father's example would foreshadow my own involvement in the PTA because he had been the President of my school's board. The notion of being involved at this level was very familiar to me.

"Of course you should chair the auction, just don't put me up front to give the speech." We were always supportive of each other and Randy was my biggest cheerleader. He was not a communicator and public speaking would have been his worst nightmare. But for me, the PTA was the perfect outlet to dedicate my time, channel my skills and remain close to my children. As a very social creature, I found myself surrounded by like-minded women who shared a common goal of enhancing our children's school while also enjoying fellowship and camaraderie. It was purposeful and fun. Once in a while Randy would complain about the tuition:

- "We have a perfectly A-rated public school in our neighborhood. Why spend the money on a private school?" He questioned wanting to make use of our tax dollars.

My comeback to him was, "What you paid for that Porsche would cover the boys' tuition for several years. I want them to be in a religious environment."

Randy was the product of excellent California public schooling. Nonetheless, once he saw for himself the loving environment at St. Paul, the daily opening of class with prayer, and the gentle affirmation of Jesus in our lives, he acknowledged, "This is not going to happen at a public school." And that was the end of the tuition payment discussion.

We were in such a good place that I decided to realize my secret dream: a third baby. I had always wanted a girl but after Michael was born our marriage was in shambles, so I gave up the notion when he was a toddler. As I neared the end of my thirties, it did not enter my mind until my best friend, Amy, got pregnant with her third child. "How about if we share the journey? Wouldn't it be fun to raise our last babies together?"

We had such a bond that she convinced me to go through this chapter with her. Randy and I tried all of the old wives' tales and tricks to conceive a daughter, but we were not surprised when the sonogram revealed another son. The older boys were thrilled at the notion of having a baby brother. At the time when Christian was born, David was eight and Michael was six years old. I would joke with Randy, "After all that you put me through, don't you dare have a mid-life crisis . . . nor are you entitled to a trophy wife. This is all you get—your trophy baby." Christian was his constant errand companion and delight. Randy enjoyed this child with the wisdom attained from having two older sons and with the leisure of them being full time in school.

...don't you dare have a mid-life crisis...
nor are you entitled to a trophy wife.

In the midst of this sunny interval in our lives, a dark cloud loomed on our horizon. When it rained, the downpour came with the vengeance of a devastating flash flood. This stemmed from a fall during one of his photo shoots. In crossing a shallow stream, Randy slipped. "Deb, I'm in a hotel and I can't get out of bed. I can't move." As he attempted to protect his cameras from falling into the water, he injured his back. For three days he lay prone, unable to move after the fall. At some later point he was prescribed some muscle relaxants and eventually graduated to painkillers to deal with his back injury.

Back in early 2000, the addictive nature of these legal drugs was not fully acknowledged, disclosed nor understood. We were oblivious he was becoming dependent on the meds. My philosophy was the body should recover naturally, remedies ought to be plant based or natural, and medication should be taken only if all else had been exhausted. Both my ancestry and my mother cemented this conviction. My grandma always carried a bottle of "Chinese Medicine"—a potent peppermint-based oil that she rubbed on any and every ailment that afflicted us. As children, we knew not to complain of a headache. If we did so, she would cluck along and pull out the bottle from her purse. When she rubbed our temples with the ointment, our eyes would sting and water up until the mint dissipated.

On the other hand, Randy would proclaim, "I am a great believer in modern medicine." He totally trusted his doctors—thinking that the right pill was a silver bullet. The notion that these prescriptions were "safe" was his prevailing thought. Sadly, we learned the hard way that internists and most doctors receive little training about addiction. For someone like Randy, the intersection of alcoholism and prescription painkillers was disastrous.

...we learned the hard way that internists and most doctors receive little training about addiction.

For a long while, we did not recognize or understand the cause and effect. All would seem well, then for no apparent reason, he would tailspin—start drinking and finally head to the ER for detox. Everything was marching along beautifully and then all of a sudden, the rug would be pulled out from under us both. Given how well we were doing as a couple, I could not bring myself to follow through with the thought of divorce—even though the final result of a "crisis" entailed uncontrollable consumption of alcohol. Leaving him was no longer an option I was willing to entertain. On the other hand, being swept away and crushed each time he succumbed to the medications and alcohol was devastating. I was not one to hide my issues, so my closest friends knew and supported me through these episodes. Although he was deeply ashamed and unwilling to divulge with our circle the cascading behavior that ended by checking into a rehab, Randy understood my need to lean on and receive emotional support from my tribe.

Being an introvert and on the quiet side, Randy's group of friends was small and also dispersed around the country. In many marriages, the husbands become friends because their wives have a relationship with each other. Randy was well liked but not well known because of his prolonged travel schedule. As we confronted the issues of addiction, his family tried to help with the best of intentions, but they were ill-equipped to be of significant support. Plus, they were in California and we were in Florida. Thus, Randy relied on me. I was his pillar.

Because of our previous counseling, our marriage was in a good place. I had relinquished control and was simply there for support or to pick up the pieces each time there was a crisis. However, I was an intensely involved wife, aware that the balance of our lives hinged on his wellbeing. I was deeply committed to figuring out what was the matter with Randy, for him, for myself and for our children. Each time he went into the vortex, he would drag me down and it was up to me to climb out—carrying both of us.

Eventually I began to observe a pattern and started to correlate these episodes with his photo shoots abroad or his visits to California. "Do you really have to go to England? I just have this feeling that you are going to return a mess." I believe the stress of being the principal figure on set and the intense physical nature of the job affected his back. While on assignment, he would use muscle relaxants to deal with the aches and pain from lugging six or more Pelican cases of heavy equipment across time zones. It was his understanding that the muscle relaxants were non-addictive, confirmed by the prescribing doctor and my research. If the discomfort did not abate, he escalated to treatment with painkillers. After flying, he invariably returned with a deep chest cold that would take weeks to work itself out. In this state, his resolve to battle the grips of addiction was severely weakened. Randy's work was physically taxing and more often than not, he would crash after a long photo shoot.

It was his understanding that the muscle relaxants were non-addictive, confirmed by the prescribing doctor and my research.

My involvement started when I'd find him either unresponsive or out of it, eyes open but holding a gaze that did not register. All he wanted to do was sleep but the incoherence of his speech and confused state was scary, so I'd rush him off to the Emergency Room. The first times I took him, I was terrified because I did not know what was happening. It was also unnerving because I had to find help to watch the children at the drop of a hat. Because he was not in critical condition, we would sometimes have to wait a long while until he was admitted. Eventually I learned to take a jacket and wear long pants since the waiting rooms are very cold. They permeate unhappiness and anxiety because anyone who steps into an ER is facing a crisis and wishes to be anywhere else but there.

Randy was in no state to explain his situation or what he had ingested so I had to piece together his medication history for admission. Sometimes I knew what he was taking but more often than not, there was a gap between my understanding and his reality. Finally, he would be wheeled into the one of the ER stalls for an IV and whatever drugs were needed to flush out his body. The first time, I returned to the waiting room and counted the hours until they released him and explained what was happening. It was during these moments of limbo that I'd ask myself, "Why?" What had we done to deserve this terrible situation? How was this going to affect our sons? The questions went unanswered and eventually I learned to stop asking my questions because there were no answers. I just had to accept the situation.

A few hours later, after being discharged, the arduous process of guarding Randy would begin for me. Even though he had been detoxed, this did not mean that the anxiety and need for the relief afforded by alcohol or the painkillers was gone. In fact, his discharge orders included further medications like Valium to manage the intense after-effects. For the non-addict, it is hard to understand how insidious and deeply seeded are these tentacles. I can only feel compassion for all who are ever in this predicament—for both the patients and their caregivers.

"Guarding" meant that I was in charge of dispensing the withdrawal meds . . . of which he could not get enough. There was no reasoning with this shadow of a man left in the shell of his body. As soon as the effects wore off, he would seek me for his next pill, regardless of the time of night. Randy was never aggressive. Instead, he was stubborn, persistent, and determined . . . giving me no peace. Even though the interval between the pills was supposed to get longer, his body had a hard time giving up the need and his spirit did not have the strength to fight. This effectively left me in charge of managing his withdrawal. As I began to familiarize myself with this cycle, it was clearly better for him to check into a rehab. He resisted all my efforts and I had to firmly stand my ground. For me, it was a choice of personifying Nurse Ratchet or the peace of knowing that someone else was in charge.

Admission to a rehab did not always turn out to be the respite I had hoped it would be. To begin, the "clients" are free to walk out at any time because they are not legally bound to remain in the center. In the beginning, as the detox cycle unfolded, Randy did not want to be there. Once he realized he could escape, he did. Much to my astonishment, he managed to walk home within a couple of hours after I had arduously cajoled him to check in. The interval between the physical detox and the mental acknowledgment to abstain is unpredictable and fragile—fraught with pitfalls to both the addict and his support system. With no experience and total ignorance of the process, I was ill-equipped to predict cause and effect because reason does not exist in this realm. I expected him to comply with the discharge instructions, but I could not fathom the insidious claws sprung by addiction nor the behavior that would ensue once it took hold of Randy.

The interval between the physical detox and the mental acknowledgment to abstain is unpredictable and fragile–fraught with pitfalls to both the addict and his support system.

Erroneously believing that alcoholism was "a thing of the past," we kept a few bottles of wine for entertaining our guests. When Randy was discharged from the hospital, we had another crisis within a few days because he used that alcohol to quench his addictions. After unexpectedly arriving at the front door after his first rehab, at the behest of our counselor Susan, I scrambled and rushed to hide the wine. As the next episodes unfolded, I learned to put away the credit cards, cash, car keys and anything that could be a means to procure more liquor. Even cough medicine was a threat, but the real culprit was not the booze, it was the painkillers. With each downfall my learning curve became steeper and equally traumatic. To this day, I am unable to remember where I've hidden things because I've had so many secret places that my memory fails me.

Once I was able to pull him through, we would do a post-mortem of all that had unfolded because Randy's memory was blurry, and I needed him to know how each scenario was upending me. He would be so dejected about his downfall and could not believe his actions. In addition to being contrite, he grew increasingly troubled at not being able to fix this problem. Always the finder of solutions, a "McGiver" of life, this one puzzle continued to elude him. For both of us, it was hard to reconcile this duality: Randy and "The Shadow."

He tried counseling, AA, medications, alternative healing, acupuncture . . . the list was growing progressively longer, but nothing seemed to work. For months at a time he would be fine and then out of the blue, we'd get blindsided with an episode. In fact, when he was "well" Randy would scoff at the notion of alcohol, saying it had no appeal to him. We could keep a few bottles of wine for months and they would go untouched. It was complicated—to say the very least—and my world started to tailspin when I got plunged into crisis mode and had to battle the Shadow. Eventually I could no longer embody "the dragon queen" and his dad had to fly out from California to intervene. I imagine this must have been a terribly conflictive moment for my father-in-law, as he confronted his own shortcomings through his son. I was beyond caring who felt what. All I wanted was for someone else be responsible for a problem that was beyond my ability to handle and was not of my making. But no one was equipped to deal with an ordeal of this magnitude.

Randy's problem was such a conundrum. Counseling had not uncovered any deep or dark secrets that might derail him in such a drastic way. Yes, he was aware and accepted the addiction problems in his family tree. He recognized his childhood was not perfect, but the therapy sessions did not reveal any deep-seated trauma. In spirit, Randy was a fun, handsome and quintessentially cool California guy with loads of drive and talent. However, his betraying body was turning him into nothing more than a druggie and a low-life loser. This laid-back SoCal boy who glowed with the western sun unwittingly ended up in the dark and twisted path of a Shakespearian drama. As each "rock bottom" got deeper, we sank to the subterranean level where we literally were pounding into hell. Nothing and no one could explain what was happening to Randy.

Early on I was oblivious to what triggered this situation, nor would I see it unfolding until it was too late. In hindsight, he was using alcohol to wean off the addictive medications. The fact that he was genetically predisposed to addiction just made for the wrong brain chemistry. Even though he successfully addressed the alcoholism, when the prescription medications came onto the scene, they proved to be much more ensnaring and dangerous. It began with the use of muscle relaxants which were NOT supposed to be addictive, cascading later with the sedatives, finally spilling over with the confluence of pain killers and alcohol. Because he trusted the medical profession and their prescriptions, he unsuspectingly became one of the early victims of the devastating painkiller wave that crested a decade or so later in the US. Even though he innocently stumbled onto this path, he quickly became experienced in learning how to get his fix. Once he succumbed to his addiction and entered Shadow mode, Randy worked the system—jumping from one walk-in clinic to the next for the prescriptions that would procure the medications.

Meanwhile, I was caught between a rock and a hard place. Randy and I had created an amazing life and I loved it. He had finally grown to be a terrific parent and was a husband who made me happy, but I was terrified of the Shadow. This specter would appear unexpectedly, and it was always extreme and increasingly trying. Every time he returned from rehab, we were both alight with hope and the promise of a new beginning. He would arm himself with more knowledge, and more therapy. He was fully committed to stay on the right path. This hope was extinguished by the next downfall, shading our future with ever growing darkness.

Every time he returned from rehab, we were both alight with hope and the promise of a new beginning.

There was one horrific incident that was incredibly upending. Although Randy had fully disclosed his addiction history, his neurologist prescribed Methadone to treat his back issues. The pain was getting so intense that he had started to consider back surgery which both of us wanted to avoid. When I researched the drug, we realized that it was a synthetic form of heroin and I called to question the doctor's office. They said this drug would not have any addictive effects on him. With their "assurances," he proceeded to start treatment but within a few days he did not like how it made him feel and he ceased taking it— without realizing that he had to taper off the amount he took. I knew something was really wrong when his pupils were different in size—one was tiny and the other was largely dilated. What a disaster.

Not having the faintest idea what tapering off meant, Randy tried to "manage" his withdrawal on his own. Because he did not want to take the pills, he turned to alcohol to wean himself. In his anxiety he once more turned to drinking which landed him again in the ER. With all of the toxicity coursing in his system, the hospital had to hook him onto a respirator to save his life because he could not breathe on his own. In essence, this is how an overdose happens. Talk about diving head onto rock bottom . . . yet another time.

In terrible desperation, I sought the Lord for strength and somehow, we got past the situation. I am grateful for the Bible studies I did at St. Paul Lutheran. They helped me grow and develop a deeper relationship with Jesus on whom I was leaning on more than ever in my life. This was when the notion of surrendering dawned on me—not as a conscious effort but as the only choice I had because I was so depleted. I prayed "Lord, PLEASE carry me through this, I. Just. Can't." And with that, I let it all go. I too had hit the bottom of my reserves and was unable to hold it all together—much less function as a mother or a wife. After that prayer, I felt like I was being lifted through a sea of quagmire in a protective cocoon that allowed me to witness but not feel. It was Peace with a capital P. Even if I could not handle my husband's issues, I was still able to mother my children.

**This was when the notion of
surrendering dawned on me–**

By the time Randy checked into what would be his final rehab experience, he had the wisdom of an old timer and the desire of a man who knows his life and his family is in the balance. His biggest fear was passing on this terrible affliction to his boys as he finally understood the genetic legacy that coursed through his DNA. When they were younger, I had protected them from witnessing their father's episodes, but as they grew older, we both were as forthcoming as we could be about drinking, pain killers and the dangers. Randy hoped that a Chinese mother with no addiction history would somewhat shield our sons from this terrible curse.

Unlike his first episodes, this one and those that followed impacted his ability to travel for work. In between the crises, I voraciously researched everything I could about the symptoms and behavior I witnessed. After observing, and educating myself, my research led me to believe that Randy suffered from hypoglycemia, which the doctors never acknowledged, but was not surprising given his alcoholism. In some obscure medical abstract, I read that the genetic markers for addiction are near the ones for diabetes and blood sugar imbalances. This made a lot of sense to me since I had seen multiple times how Randy would pass out within the hour of treating the boys (and himself) a sugar loaded Seven/Eleven Slurpee. It was unquestionable that he had addiction in his genes.

In parallel, I had become disturbingly familiar with Soma, Lexapro, Percocet, Oxycodone, Naproxen, Vicodin, Xanax, Valium . . . the list was extensive. I had never taken any medication in my life, but I was on a first-name basis with these pills and it was an unwelcome relationship.

Instead, I opted to prepare meals that would support his health, cooking like a fiend and adopting a low carb diet before it was even a trend. My highly multicultural heritage allowed for a widely varied arsenal of meal options: Asian, West Indies, Mexican, Caribbean, etc. I educated myself on alternative healing options and researched all that had to do with his condition. With each occurrence, I became progressively more distrustful of the prescription drugs.

After the respirator and the rehab that followed, we both acknowledged that everything had to change. In a moment of deep despair, Randy said to me, "Deb, what else can I do? Maybe it would have been better for you if I had died." Randy had a strong will to live but he could not fathom why he kept slipping and what was wrong with him. He was tortured by how much we both had suffered and how each crisis affected our sons. They were old enough to know something was wrong and had begun to witness his demise. He did not want them to be scarred by his downfall and affected by his addiction. As we clung to each other with tears streaming down our faces, I told Randy, "There has got to be a way to beat this. We have to fight this. I'm not going to let you die."

Given the generous royalties we collected from his life's work, we had the option of pairing down the travel and of declining the huge funded productions which added so much stress to his life. I blamed his work and begged him to walk away from it all. For most men, this would be a bitter pill to swallow, but his health (or lack of it) was making this his only choice. He was now under the care of a psychiatrist and was taking a host of meds to help his anxiety and depression which was the latest diagnosis.

**For most men, this would be a bitter pill to swallow,
but his health (or lack of it)
was making this his only choice.**

I was appalled at the horse-sized pills they prescribed, but since they were not opiates, I left Randy's health up to the experts. "Deb, you know, I have all the symptoms of depression, but I don't feel sad." Randy had finally learned to be in touch with his feelings and his health. He was able to acknowledge the heart palpitations, tiredness, sleepiness . . . and note the absence of sadness. He was the eternal optimist, so it was intensely distressing to see him as a shadow of the person I knew. He had lost 30 pounds which was significant since he was already fit and slim. His strength had waned, and he was gaunt and pale. The twinkle in his eyes was missing as was his drive and love for life.

We both worked for months at nursing his health. It was markedly easier from an emotional perspective because we were both on the same page, spurred by the common goal of getting better and returning us to normal. Although he was on a heavy cocktail of prescription drugs from his psychiatrist, Randy was no longer taking pain meds or turning to the bottle as an option if they became unmanageable. A visit to the internist revealed somewhat high cholesterol levels but given the pressing issue of generalized anxiety and tiredness, the doctor did not think this was urgent and said we would look into that at the next follow-up scheduled months ahead.

Randy rested, helped with the kids when they came back from school and then he rested again. The only time he would rally was for the boys—to either take them to Boy Scouts or any of their after-school activities. It was a supreme juggling act to carry the load of three young boys, care for a sick husband and finish my PTA President term. Much before the ventilator drama, I had risen up the ranks and been installed President Elect. "It's an honor but I must decline. We just have too much going on." Randy said, "Deb, I think you'd be great at being President. Do it!" He cheered me on and encouraged my acceptance. In the end, according to the bylaws, I was the only board member that fit the requirements for the role. With confidence in having a phenomenal team to lead—and delegate, I took on the responsibilities.

All of the work that I did for St. Paul Lutheran School, the relationships I forged, and the funds I helped to raise would come to bear fruits in ways that I would never have anticipated. For sure, I was happy to volunteer my abilities and our money to this parochial community. Randy used to remark that after all we had contributed, tuition should be free. Unbeknownst to me, I was developing a network that was soon going to carry our family through its hardest moments.

And so in 2009, after a quiet and restful summer, color finally returned to Randy's face and he started to behave more like himself. He wanted to build things and do projects around the house. I was cautiously optimistic. I will never forget our last meaningful conversation as we rode in his convertible, "If this was all I have, I am totally satisfied with life. All I want for our future is for you to be happy and to watch the boys grow up. I've achieved everything I could ever imagine." Along with the amazing heights he had experienced, life had dealt him some terrible blows. He was always so remorseful about the distress his episodes caused us, but he was grateful for my support and steadfast loyalty. He had achieved professionally beyond his wildest dreams and he could do without all of the extra properties, cars and toys. We had all we needed: each other, our kids, and our health.

That conversation brings peace to my heart when I remember it. I feel certain that Randy was at the peak of his best emotional self. Despite all that had transpired, he was living in gratitude, love, and faith. After all the challenges we faced together, we had come full circle in our relationship. No longer naïve about life, our marriage had survived—despite all of the trials that life had hurled at us. The love that we felt as a young couple had matured and seen us through all of the very high highs and the low bottoms of our journey together. That big black clay pot from Oaxaca that he bought when we first met had cracked after baby Christian inadvertently pushed it. We were devastated to see it shattered in pieces, but I carefully glued it back together. "This pot is a metaphor of our marriage: broken, no longer perfect and marred but I pieced it together!" I made this remark tongue in cheek. "Look, it's still standing. And it is beautiful if you don't look too closely!"

It was October of 2009. Randy was cheerful, finally feeling healthy and ready to tackle life once again. I had just experienced my first season as a fashion consultant. Because of all my connections and "mom chic" style, a close friend recruited me to take over an existing franchise and represent a high-end fashion line called ETCETERA. I would set up my home like a boutique and sell through private appointments. LeeAnne, my manager and friend, trained me in sales while Randy and I watched, "What Not to Wear" and read "Color Me Beautiful" so I could learn my new craft. It was fun and fascinating. And it provided much needed frivolity from the doldrum of the prior months. "Deb, after you've given so much of yourself volunteering, it is time that you had something of your own." Randy was very excited for me. He was "over-the-top" encouraging—showing his support by taking care of the three boys 'round the clock as I set up my shop and tended to my customers.

When Randy expressed wanting to travel to California, fear gripped me. I was adamantly against him doing any travel. Just the notion of returning to the darkness of his anxiety, depression, and possible relapse was paralyzing. Even though we were talking like reasonable adults, what I really wanted to do was chain him to a chair, snap on a padlock and throw away the key. I felt like saying, "Are. You. Kidding? What are you thinking? I just KNOW you will come back from California a mess." Instead, I calmly asked, "Do you really think this is a good idea? Why is this trip necessary?"

**Just the notion of returning to the darkness
of his anxiety, depression,
and possible relapse was paralyzing.**

His answer was, "This is merely exploratory—no work is involved. Plus, I want to give the boat a look over, check on the beach house and negotiate refinancing terms. It will not be stressful."

Even though a feeling of aversion and fear nestled in my gut, I really could not conjure up a logical explanation to keep him in Florida. We both were on the quest to go back to life as we knew it. Our desire to normalize our existence overrode my concerns. I did not want to be the gust of wind that blew out his hopeful little flame. Against my better instincts, I acquiesced, drove him to the airport, and kissed him goodbye.

**Our desire to normalize our
existence overrode my concerns.
I did not want to be the gust of wind
that blew out his hopeful little flame.**

A few days into his trip, I could hear it in his voice as we spoke—something was off. I panicked and insisted that he return to Florida before it was too late. By then, I was so familiar with the downward spiral that I knew how he would collapse—line by line—like the actress who has memorized the playbook by heart. My nerves started to unravel, and I braced myself to receive the next impact.

When I picked him up at the airport, I could see it in his eyes and his demeanor. He was predictably tired, lifeless and sick. Whatever optimism had blossomed over the summer was quashed for both of us. The flame of hope was snuffed out. Randy could feel the draining of his body while the foreboding sensation of defeat washed over me. I was deflated and again, I found myself resigned to play the role of the nurse and caretaker.

Into the Furnace

"Gold is tested by fire. People by God."

Chinese Proverb

For those who are hearing this news for the first time, Randy has been in the hospital since last Wednesday. We went to the ER to stitch up a cut on his eyebrow due to a fall. Since then, we have learned that he has acute kidney failure and some other liver condition (rhabdomyolysis). In the course of trying to determine why, a CT scan revealed nodules in his lungs. Not good.

How quickly life can change…at the drop of a hat. Something happens that rearranges all of our priorities. What is seemingly important is suddenly trivial and what we thought mattered at one moment is rapidly forgotten. On the Wednesday (right before Thanksgiving), I found Randy laying on the garage floor, unable to move.

Our son David loves to cook, and he was busy preparing his first full-on Thanksgiving meal. Yes, only 10 years old and already he was capable of delivering a standing rib roast, a turkey, and pies. I, of course, was busily doubling as sous chef and clean-up crew, so I did not notice Randy's absence. He had been on the floor for hours, but he was too weak to call out. When I found him, I tried to get him to stand up, but his knees buckled and his legs were not functioning.

In the beginning, I thought he had relapsed. He was drawn, tired and any advances into his recovery were set back after returning from California. My past experience had taught me these were the ideal conditions to trigger a relapse—when his physical and mental state were at their weakest. It did not occur to me to call 911. Partly because in Latin America, you usually get yourself to the hospital and partly because I was so programmed to deal with everything on my own. I don't know where I found the strength, but I hauled him into the car and raced to the hospital.

I went from fretting that we did not spend Thanksgiving together— celebrating David's talents—to facing a prolonged hospitalization. As the doctors delivered the diagnosis of his condition, their whispers hinting the big "C-word" started getting louder and our life began to implode. Cancer. I could not begin to think about the implications. I could only begin living hour by hour as I defaulted to my autopilot mode. I needed to keep calm for the kids, pretend to be calm for Randy, as well as organize and review the tasks at hand. I also needed to ask for help.

Simply having the time to be at the hospital required my engineering degree to plan out a schedule which included meeting the bare minimum needs for three little boys. As the situation unfolded into "code red" for our family, an army of friends and neighbors started getting involved to lend a helping hand. They babysat, shuttled my kids around, or left meals on our front porch. It was a blessing not to shop or prepare food because life came to a screeching halt. All that mattered was getting to the hospital, meeting with the doctors and researching the options. I thought if I could understand all of the possibilities, that would give me a handle on our lives.

This crisis was unlike anything I had ever faced. After several rehabs and that latest ventilator incident, I thought I had nerves of steel and could handle ANYTHING. In the past I would have reached out to my tribe to vent and talk things out. This time, I did not have the luxury of making such phone calls because everything was happening too quickly. Prior to blogs, I just needed to keep up with my support system—to remain connected with the many friends who were helping and were concerned. My best option was to send nightly emails. Even though this writing was mainly intended to update them with new information or ask for help, somehow these messages were also a reality check. They brought a semblance of order to my thoughts. My writing was therapeutic.

December 1st, 2009

Firstly, I would like to thank all of you for your words, sentiments of support and helping hands. All things considered, I feel like your prayers are keeping our family within a relatively "normal" state of being and I myself am very calm and serene at the moment. Only through the grace of God are we getting through this difficult time. I am starting to reach out as needed. Even if I do not get to you, know that I appreciate your concerns and goodwill.

My window to see Randy in the morning was tighter than a crammed bookshelf. While the older boys were in school, Christian was still a noon-napping toddler. "We must not drop the nap" I would mutter to myself. I knew the collision of dinner, bath and bedtime for three kids with only one parent to handle it all was nerve-wracking. A cranky toddler was the straw that would break this camel's back. Given Randy's prolonged absences abroad, I was an expert at the single mom rodeo and knew my limitations. I was rigid about the nap because I needed the time to breathe without a toddler at my heels. That was the only slot in our routine that still kept its place as everything else was quickly becoming irrelevant.

Although the original reason for rushing off to the hospital was a cut on his eyebrow that looked deep enough to warrant stitches, this quickly became the minor issue. It was absolutely insignificant compared to what else was coming down the pike. The first tests revealed a high level of white blood cells which signaled a major infection. In the course of determining what was going on, I was told that his kidneys had shut down and that he had developed rhabdomyolysis. As if that was not enough, his liver enzymes were abnormal, and Randy was starting to turn yellow. To cap it all, a CT scan revealed several nodules in his lungs. Even though Randy continued to be out of it, clearly this was not a disappointing relapse, but it was something much more complicated and devastating.

The medical report was laying on the hospital counter, so I opened it furtively to understand why a particular nodule in his lungs was of concern. I felt as if I was committing industrial espionage, but the doctors were not entirely forthcoming in their updates. They delivered the results with barely any emotion and gave me little time to process or ask questions. I felt like I was imposing on their precious time. A medical degree was not necessary for me to jump to conclusions when hearing the words "nodules" and "lungs" in the same sentence. With the specter of cancer looming over us, I needed more information to somehow bring a semblance of understanding over a situation that was clearly beyond the boundaries of anything we had ever imagined. I leafed through the pages until I found what I was looking for. The nodule was amorphous and larger than the others found in his X-ray. They were hoping this would explain Randy's kidney shut down.

December 1st, 2009 (cont.)

Brain, abdomen and all other organs are clear of any tumors or masses. Lung nodules are indicative of a metastasis. In other words, they would be secondary. Hoping the colonoscopy will yield nothing significant—therefore no primary source.

Once the kids were tucked away for the night I'd rush out to the hospital once again, when my neighbor came over to babysit. In one of those coming and goings I was so immersed in my own thoughts that I ran a stop sign and went over the speed limit . . . all witnessed by the police car tucked away in the shadows. "Officer, I think my husband has cancer." One look at my face and a near to tears explanation was all the officer needed to let me off the hook—a small mercy in my time of despair. Even though I was usually at the hospital three times a day, I felt this was not enough. The life of the man I loved, the father of my children, was in the balance. My self-expectations were simply not humanly possible to accomplish, but I kept on trying. Visiting hours ended at 10:00 p.m. so when I returned home, I researched until exhaustion put me to sleep. I became extremely proficient on Google—my new best friend—we visited every night and stayed up late together.

Preparing for the colonoscopy had drained his already weakened body. Randy was exhausted from the experience which was nothing short of unpleasant. He was slowly recovering and his general appearance was improving. Because of all the IV fluids, his face had lost its haggardness and his wrinkles had filled up. The black eye caused by his fall was almost gone and his eyebrow stitches had been removed. "Wow, you look like you've had a mini face lift. And you don't look like a pirate anymore!" I quipped, trying to make light out of an impossibly heavy situation.

December 1st, 2009 (Late Evening Update)

Good news regarding the colonoscopy. They found nothing of consequence which makes me optimistic that the nodules are caused by bacteria or fungus picked up from one of Randy's many trips. The next step is the lung biopsy which will hopefully confirm this line of thought.

Randy was not one to ask many questions which allowed me to avoid disclosing any details about his lung nodules. He did not ask, so I did not tell as I tiptoed explaining the prolonged hospitalization that was leading up to the lung biopsy. He was physically looking more like himself but as his appearance improved, so did his awareness. Because of the high levels of enzymes and off-balance body chemistry, he had been out of it until this moment. As his levels were returning to normality, his dream state was replaced by the cognition that this hospitalization had severe implications. As he came to himself, anxiety started to take hold of him.

When he was well enough to be fed up about being hospitalized, he insisted on escaping while I tried to convince him that staying was necessary. Finally, I had no choice but to come clean about the possibility of cancer. I think he probably knew more than he was letting on, but he had defaulted to denial as long as possible. As our wills battled each other, I found myself requesting via e-mail that my prayer warriors ask for Randy's serenity and peace of mind.

"Randy, you need to find some way to calm yourself and keep still so I can do the heavy lifting." In reality, what I felt like saying was "In this canoe, you need to SIT down, STOP moving, and let me paddle so I can get the five of us out of this swamp. Do NOT rock the boat."

When we were together in the cold hospital room, we did not say much to each other. After having been through the wringer and beyond, we could sit and just be. Ten years prior, I remember being perched by a window table at "The Lord Nelson"—Australia's oldest pub. We were surrounded by the beauty of Sydney's harbor when we "coincided" in our travels for work (Randy made that happen). We sat in silence and contentment of being in each other's company. "We are like two old people who don't have anything to say to each other" he remarked —even though I had yet to celebrate my 30th birthday. Much had changed since those days. Though my presence broke the monotony of his hospitalization, I had so much on my plate that relaxing was supremely difficult. When I was not with him, I would juggle to get to the hospital but as I sat with Randy, all I could think of was everything that remained undone at home.

Somehow the mundane tasks such as meals and laundry were happening while homework and cleaning went by the wayside. I lack a photographic memory, so my neatness and organization were tools to avert the insanity of trying to find misplaced items. With all that was happening, it was obvious that our home was starting to look like a disaster zone and that my life was slowly following the state of our house.

December 4, 2009

The surgeon wants Randy's kidneys to be more stable before he does the biopsy. It will probably be one or two more days of waiting. This is getting on our nerves, but we are dealing with it. With every system/organ being checked off one by one, the likelihood of the nodules being malignant is diminishing, giving us the optimism to assume that they are coming from a bacterial or fungal source.

As a seasoned project manager, I could not help but be concerned about the medical care that my husband was receiving. I asked myself: If he is the project, who is the manager? Theoretically there was a general MD who oversaw his case, but with the multiple organs and specialists involved, I could not see clear lines of communication. Does anyone fully know what is going on with Randy? Is anyone looking at the whole person?

Clearly, my husband was in no position to make decisions for himself. If he were alone in this world, who would advocate for him? It was a sobering thought to realize how much he depended on me. I tried to be on my A-game and show up at the hospital when the doctors made their rounds. I wanted to be prepared and ask intelligent questions, but with the logistics of a young family, I was barely able to keep this ship afloat. "Sapped and bone tired" fell short of describing my state of mind and being.

Randy had nothing but time on his hands as he convalesced. He was fully lucid, very aware and bored out of his mind. Meanwhile, every second of my day was scheduled. I was the one immersed in the results and details. One of my friends who had been in the eye of a storm herself, said to me, "Do yourself a favor and keep a notebook with the names of the MD's, conditions described, medications taken, and indications given." All of the information being hurled at me was hugely overwhelming. I carried my book with all of the time, my notes were scribbled all over the margins. Every bit of data was plastered onto those pages. It was my brain drain. I no longer communicated with Randy. My notebook took his place and it was the recipient of the facts, my thoughts, and our fears. It was heavy. This concrete and tangible bunch of papers was my reference, my personal diary and my medical Bible.

My friends in Mexico and Panama prayed for us. "Deb, I am so frustrated—there isn't anything I can do for you at this critical time." I knew that their prayers were keeping us above water. There was no other explanation. Despite the situation, I was surprisingly efficient and calm. However, my pendulum swung between having "nerves of steel" to total numbness. I had navigated the rehab circuit so I was an expert at operating in crisis mode. Nonetheless, this was like landing a part on Broadway when all you've done is regional theater. I was out of my league. Their prayers coated my anxiety like a soothing balm and finally, I was able to sleep restfully because my mind was not racing. I should have been on the verge of a breakdown, but the prayers were keeping me away from the edge of the abyss.

December 4th, 2009 (Evening)

First is the Lord. It is through His grace that we can go through these experiences in life without basically losing our sanity. Therefore, most important are the prayers that come from the hearts of our family and friends. What you are doing for us with your spirit and soul is equally as important as the physical and mental help that my friends here in Boca are providing us. Please keep on praying for us.

We are truly blessed to have this village taking care of our needs. If there were ever a textbook case of a community coming together to see us through a crisis, this would be the perfect example. Thanks again, and if you wish to forward this mail onto anyone that I may have omitted or who would like to keep abreast of the situation, please feel free to do so. There are no worries about HIPPA here!

The village. Never did I anticipate that all those years of volunteer work would yield such fruit for our family. As we talked about the help we received, Randy was in awe of the sheer number of people that were supporting us in many ways (about 30). The long hours of convalescence afforded him a lot of time to think and ponder. At one point he remarked, "Deb, I'm happy to take this one for the team'" He knew that I was mentally strong but physically weak. That he could not juggle life like I did, and if one of us had to endure this hospitalization, he'd rather be the one. As he expressed his gratitude, I could not help but think to myself: What if it IS cancer? How. Am. I … going to do this?

December 7th, 2009

Ladies, thank you so much for watching Christian, my shy baby. I'm surprised that he has gone without a single tear to so many babysitters … and obviously he has had a great time. More than once he has awakened from his nap to complete strangers (no offense to Bonnie and Jackie!). Because of your help, Randy's day is much more palatable. We walk together and by now know all of the elevator locations and corridors. Randy makes about 10 rounds a day to keep his blood flowing and his sanity somewhat intact.

As Randy regained his strength, we walked the corridors of the hospital together. Waiting. Waiting for results. Waiting for answers. Waiting for the next step, which was the biopsy. In my heart, I knew it was not cancer, but Randy was masterfully hiding his anxiety about the possibility. He was the eternal optimist, but he must have been scared. I was too tired to even think about it, and I was certain it would not be cancer just because I could not continue to burn both ends of the candle. Cancer could not happen to us. My mind simply could not absorb the possibility of another life-altering health trauma.

So, we walked to pass the time, to move the blood, to keep him sane. "Deb, my floor is awful. I don't know why I'm here but it's a nightmare."

He was on the geriatric floor. Most of the patients were senile or had memory loss. They would wake up screaming and wailing because they did not know where they were, or they had forgotten the circumstances that brought them to the hospital. Randy was horrified and should not have been on this floor. Our conversation went something like this:

"Please get me out of here."

"You need to hold it together until your numbers are good enough for the biopsy."

"I can't stand this any longer. I need to leave."

"If you leave now, I doubt the insurance will cover the biopsy at a later date. You've got to be patient. This IS the best option."

We also discussed the inevitable pain after the procedure and the drugs that would follow. I explained to the doctor that my husband had a history of addiction. I described how bad it was and I told him it was a door that we did not want to open.

He replied, "Mrs. Faris, we want to get to the bottom of this, so we need to perform the lung biopsy."

There was no easy option. Truly, we did not have a choice. His surgery needed to proceed.

December 8th, 2009

Well, tomorrow is the big day. Randy goes in at 10:30 for the lung biopsy. The surgeon will try to get the sample from one incision, using a guided lighted wire. If this procedure is not satisfactory, he may have to make a second incision. Perhaps, even a third incision might be necessary. They need to get a good enough chunk of the lung to yield conclusive findings. The results will not be known for another 5-7 days. Randy is nervous about a multitude of things— the surgery, the anesthesia, the results. I've tried to keep his spirits up, but I think at this point, your prayers will do him better as I am very weary and depleted.

P.S. Lauren, your dinner was such a hit with the boys. They love anything to do with pasta (must be the Italian in me — ha, ha!).

I went to the hospital before the lung biopsy and we sat together, waiting. For once, our roles were reversed. I was in blissful denial and he was truly scared. In my soul, I knew this was not cancer. There was no rhyme or reason. I simply did not entertain the possibility. We both were consumed by our own thoughts as we prayed together and held hands before they prepped Randy for the procedure. As they wheeled him out, I said goodbye and left for home.

The typical thing is to sit and wait for news from the operating surgeon, but this was not my reality. In my world, time to sit was a non-existent commodity—a luxury I could not afford. I ran off to take care of the rest of my household.

December 9th, 2009

I just got the call from the lung surgeon. Randy did very well during the procedure. He is now in recovery and they were able to get a good sample. Although we will not have the results for several days, he told me that it is highly unlikely that there is any cancer, and what he found probably stemmed from some infection or tropical disease. This surgeon is extremely cautious and does not go out on a limb. Therefore, his feedback is surprising and wonderful.

Thank you for all your prayers which have kept us sane and serene during all of these days. A few of you have commented on how gracefully I am getting through this and keeping it all together. I can only witness that it is only through the grace of God that we are walking through this experience. Your prayers are very much being felt by our family.

My young, handsome, and full of life husband who used to be strong like an ox, had aged physically and mentally during this time—especially since the ventilator incident. He began to lean on me more and more. I took care of his health. I took care of the kids. I took care of our house. Doing it all was breaking me down, but I found solace and peace knowing how much Randy appreciated me.

He was gratified to have chosen, pursued and married a woman of substance, strength, and capability. Although he was quiet and shy, in the recent years he was very expressive to the boys about his admiration and respect towards me. I knew beyond a shadow of a doubt that he was thankful I stood by his side and he could rely on me. He was completely confident that, as his marriage partner, I could pull this off and he was relieved to have placed his trust in me. It was a far departure from the years when our marriage was in jeopardy and when I felt unappreciated and undervalued.

Because we started to make so much money quickly and when we were young, for a while Randy became enthralled with the material things—fast cars and beautiful boats. However, in the last year I knew he found peace with who he was and what he had: his wife and his children. He loved me and he loved his boys. I am comforted knowing that he was living in a state of gratitude and emotional harmony.

With the biopsy behind us, we started to prepare for Randy's release after 15 days in the hospital. It was surreal that we had been through this ordeal in just over two weeks. I was drained. Christmas was around the corner and the kids would be on vacation. I knew I'd be caring for my sick husband. Our emotions were very different. He was thankful to put the experience behind us and was looking forward to normalcy. I, however, was dreading what might lay ahead.

As we prepared for his release, I asked the nephrologist: "What if the lung condition is unrelated to the kidney shut down? What then?" My logic told me that should a cause for the kidney failure remain unexplained, this nightmare would repeat itself all over again. His reply was rather flippant: "We are not CSI." So, how would I know what to do? Where did this leave me? His answer was "It may happen again; you'll see it coming." His answer was unhelpful and uncaring. It also was insulting to my intelligence in every shape and form. I felt like telling him, "Yes, you are CSI: Conceited, Snide and Insensitive!"

The combination of multiple layers of health problems, lack of cohesion from the doctors, and Randy's past addiction issues, was akin to patching up his health with duct tape—hoping their diagnosis would somehow stick, seal and mend. Ironically, Randy was a modern-day MacGyver, a jack of all trades that could fix it all with his ingenuity and inventiveness. He always kept of roll of duct tape handy which according to him, could repair anything. I was not entirely convinced of the solutions outlined by the doctors, but I had little choice other than to follow their plan.

December 10th, 2009

Randy is finally home. Other than feeling as if he had an awful chest cramp, he is doing as well as can be expected. Last night was brutal, like having four candles lit onto his back.

Once the drainage tube was yanked out of his side—yes, yanked or ripped would be the right term—the pain lessened considerably. We still do not have answers but for now, we are simply relieved that the nodules did not look malignant.

Life should begin to resume its normalcy—this has been rather surreal. It was weird walking out of Boca Community for a last time. I am looking forward to getting into Christmas mode. This year we will relish it with a different feel.

So many people helped us through this ordeal—some were close to us, others simply were giving members of the St. Paul community. We even had friends help us set up our Christmas tree. I remember thinking, "When I get past this episode, I hope it will be like childbirth: I will forget the pain and anxiety and remember the joy of love, help and generosity."

Randy was weak, very weak. During the mornings he would either sleep or rest and rally when the kids arrived from school. They were happy he was around. They saw the wounds and watched him perform breathing exercises to keep his lungs from collapsing. Somehow, as traumatic as it was for me, I had spared the boys from the magnitude of this ordeal. They had visited the hospital a few times but other than that, life appeared normal to them. We attended the school Christmas concert together and people wished us well. Randy put up a good front, but the twinkle in his eyes was gone.

December 18th, 2009

It is official. The nodules are not cancerous, but they have a fungal origin. This news has given Randy much relief and peace of mind. He has been feeling rather tired and he has had more pain than in previous days since he stopped taking the medication. He is still very much in recovery mode and not sleeping properly. He wakes up at 4:00 am which is when they would come to take blood at the hospital. It seems that it is going to take a while before he is healthy again.

I am so glad I've kept this account because Randy has read it and sees how much help we have all received from your caring and generosity. Since Christmas cards will not be going out this year, please receive our love and thoughts during this season as we have surely felt yours.

Randy was tired and hurting. I helped him to deal with the pain medication and the withdrawal effects which concerned us both. He was so relieved not to have cancer. This second brush with mortality was very scary. Until this crisis, he was always positive or wore the mantle of denial like a pro. His grandma lived until she was practically 100 years old, so he expected to live longer than most. On the other hand, my grandma and 5 of her siblings had died from the big C—most of them were quite young. In the days when even saying the word Cancer was practically a taboo, my mother had grown up with this shadow looming over her family. Because of its devastating prevalence in my ancestry, I envisioned myself as the first to go. I told Randy, "After all the ministering and nursing that I have lavished upon you, I hope you take care of me as well when it's my turn." He thought I was joking but I'm not a funny person. I was dead serious.

Growing up in tropical Latin America, our "seasons" were punctuated by either the rainy months or the dry ones. But Christmas always marked a time for celebration and was the unveiling of many traditions involving food, songs, and décor—so it was always my favorite time of the year. We had a great Christmas and we were so blessed to have this special interlude together. The kids were enjoying themselves and we were slowly getting back into our new normal state of life in between the medical appointments.

It would be wishful thinking to imagine that I was operating with my senses at full capacity. I was definitely sleep deprived, high strung, and seeking relief. Months before, my family had booked a cruise that sailed on January 2nd. My parents, brother, his fiancée and our family would all join together on the voyage. Despite everything that had happened with Randy, we were still looking forward to this get away. In retrospect, the idea that he could travel and be out in the middle of the ocean was ludicrous, but such was my mental disarray that I plunged ahead as if this was really going to happen. I just so wanted a break from keeping everyone fed . . . and alive. Between Christmas and New Year's, it was a crazy week trying to nail Randy's follow-up medical appointments, but we needed to have the action plan before sailing away. We were also still looking for answers.

December 24th, 2009

The fungus has a name: Histoplasmosis. It's mostly found in caves with bat guano. Where, when, and how Randy acquired it is an unresolved mystery. He could have acquired it this past summer when we were in Panama or maybe 20 years ago. This condition is unrelated to his whole kidney problem. It was simply discovered along the way and presented the cancer scare. It should be treated once we get some blood work done, but it is not urgent. If anyone has some thoughts on this subject, we would appreciate your knowledge.

With the histoplasmosis diagnosed, we visited the infectious disease doctor who prescribed a course of pretty serious medications for treatment. This fungus explained why Randy would easily contract any of the colds du jour. He always returned sick from his travels (I think the poor air quality of the flights was the culprit), and his colds would take longer than normal to overcome with coughs deeply imbedded in his chest. Our next step was the appointment with the internist. The physicians all work independently from each other, as if each body part was a separate state with its own borders. Observing the lack of cohesion from the doctors, my trust was further eroding. I was not confident they were looking at Randy as a whole human being. Instead, I had become the glue that was keeping it all together.

Randy's medications had to be carefully monitored to avert any harmful interactions. So much had been prescribed to him over the last few years that I could not fathom who was going to manage it nor how it was going to work out for him. Despite the prognosis that eliminated cancer as a possibility, nothing had truly explained the kidney shut down which was the original dilemma. His issues were a knot inserted into a conundrum—layers of problems that had not been diagnosed to the satisfaction of my inquiring mind.

I suspected his kidneys were working overtime filtering out all of the prescribed pills, but none of the doctors endorsed my theory. I knew it would be several long weeks before Randy was once again healthy and could assume his natural role in our family: to be the husband and father that he wanted to be. Given all of the unanswered questions that nagged at me and kept me on edge, I felt the need to laugh and forget. I wanted to escape for a few hours, so I made plans.

December 29th, 2009

Ladies, Amy and I are going to get together this evening for a well-deserved "girls night out." We are planning to dine together and later catch a movie. There are several good ones we could see:

It's complicated (with Meryl Streep)

Nine (all the women)

Up in the Air (with George Clooney—eye candy anyone?)

Would love if you can join us for all or part of the evening.

Looking forward to seeing you!

Debbie

We chose to see "It's complicated." It was such a funny movie. I laughed so much. My night out was a great distraction and I spent a lovely evening with the girls. Thank goodness for these ladies who could really commiserate with me. Who needs a therapist when I was surrounded by the best listening ears and the finest prayerful hearts?

On the morning of December 30st I woke up to a husband who was clearly "out of it" again. I experienced that sinking feeling in my gut that was disturbingly familiar. In fact, the feeling was so familiar that for a brief moment, I felt like brushing it off. But the sailing date for the cruise was nearing and the words of the discharging nephrologist haunted me, "You'll see it coming." I feared the recurrence of a bad kidney, so we marched back to the hospital emergency room.

Upon admission, Randy could not recall our eldest son's name nor the US President at the time. He was already weak but now he was also dazed and confused. Upon entering the ER they ran a battery of tests while I waited outside, feeling cold and miserable. Thoughts that I had stuffed away since my movie night reared their unwelcome heads once more. After a few hours the results were favorable enough to release him, but their explanation was inconclusive. Perhaps the strain his body had sustained in the past few weeks had weakened him. "No, Mrs. Faris, he does not have kidney failure, they are working just fine."

By the end of the day, Randy was back to himself and the thought of spending another minute at the hospital was traumatic. "Deb, I want to go home." Any other time I would have put up a fight and questioned this outcome because what I had observed did not make sense. At that moment, however, I was defeated and outnumbered: he wanted to leave and the hospital staff wanted us to go. I was in Randy's corner, but no one was in mine, so we departed without good answers, simply hoping for the best.

We returned home early evening and my only thought was to feed Randy and go to bed. He did not even want to eat, but his weakened stomach was empty since the day before, so I heated up some soup. As I fed him, he looked into my eyes and acknowledged the weariness that had etched itself on my face. "Deb, don't worry. Everything will be all right." These were the last words he ever said to me.

December 31,2009

This is Debbie's dad. Since Debbie has been keeping you all informed regarding the state of Randy's health, I am taking the liberty of regretfully informing you that Randy passed away this morning. Yesterday, he was taken to the hospital since Debbie feared a recurrence of his previous condition when she found him extremely weak and incoherent. After being checked and blood samples analyzed, there was no indication of either his kidney or his liver acting up again and he was released. The doctors felt that due to his immune system being so low, and the trauma that his body had been subjected to, his recovery time would be lengthy, and on this note he was allowed to come home.

He spent the day in bed, extremely tired but coherent. In the evening Debbie fed him some supper and he went back to sleep. This morning at 8:17, when Debbie woke up, she could not awaken him and 911 was called immediately. We were told that he passed away in his sleep several hours before. At the moment, his body has been transferred to the medical examiner's laboratory for an autopsy, given the fact that he had been released from the hospital less than 24 hours before his demise. No arrangements have been made at this time for any services, pending the release of his body and the arrival of his family, complicated by the time of the year. Many of you have already been informed of all of this, but we wanted to make sure that everyone on Debbie's list knew the latest— especially since you have all been so supportive during the last weeks. Debbie's mom, her brother and myself would like to thank you all for being such special friends of Debbie, and for all the help that she has received. Friends and family like you, are so very important at moments like these, and we are very appreciative for all you have done for Debbie.

Thank you and God bless you all,
Eugene and Joanne

And this is how on the last day of 2009, I was ushered into another unwanted chapter of my life. I did not even want to read this book— much less be a character in this novel— and yet I had no choice. I had become the lead in this tragedy of a story.

Crossing the
Threshold of Never

The paramedics came almost instantly, within 5 minutes of my call. They entered our bedroom and soon after told me that Randy had died in his sleep. I was numb. Somehow the police also arrived. They took my statement. I remember feeling oddly detached as I told them what had happened in the last 24 hours, but as I heard myself recount the chain of events, the growing need of an explanation overshadowed any other emotion. "Mrs. Faris, we may need to conduct an autopsy, are you OK with this?" I stared at the officer incredulously: "Of course I want an autopsy. In fact, I DEMAND an autopsy." This was not supposed to happen, not after they said he was OK. "We JUST were at the hospital. This can't be possible."

I don't know who told David, our eldest, but I could hear him sobbing loudly in the other room. I remember seeing the confusion in Michael's little face whereas the baby was oblivious. "Get them out of the house. Take them to the movies" I said to my brother because I did

125

not want them to witness what was happening that morning, nor was I able to cope with them. For the first time in my life, I shunned being emotionally present for my boys. Lost to me was the ability to feel empathy—even for my own children, David, Michael and Christian. My own pain was so overwhelming that it blocked out anything else. I had started to withdraw from life as I knew it.

Despite the density of my confusion, I had a moment of clarity and the presence of mind to call the doctor who oversaw Randy's case at the hospital. Thank goodness for my notebook with all of its annotations because it gave me the semblance of still being in charge of Randy's health. The truth, however, was that I was about to abandon that role forever. The doctor had nothing to say and could offer no other explanations except her deep sympathy. Shock started to set in, replacing the numbness. I locked myself in the baby's room, called my best friend Amy, and after two hours of keeping myself together I finally fell apart.

I only remember vague bits and pieces of that first day: stunned friends coming by to see me; my neighbor sending over a huge sandwich platter; surrounding Randy's body to pray right before the paramedics put him on a stretcher and took him away. As they wheeled him out of the house, I shut my eyes and held hands with my girlfriends who shielded my view. I did not want that to be my last memory of Randy.

Crying. I was crying so much that I could not see through my eyes. My lids were so swollen that my face was disfigured. My almond-shaped eyes were distorted into abnormal slivers that were barely open. Word got around pretty quickly, so friends came over and we sobbed together. There was one brief glimmer of light when one of my friends shared that her mother, who was three times widowed, had been visited by two of her deceased husbands when she slept. These had been comforting experiences to her. I desperately clung to that possibility because I felt utterly devastated and horribly alone. I wanted to see Randy again. If I was emotionally depleted from the hospital ordeal since Thanksgiving, now I was below empty, in the negative, with nothing left inside of me. It felt like my entrails were torn and ripped out of me.

In my prior adversities I would beseech: "Dear God, please help us through this trial" or "Dear Jesus, please let the surgery be successful." From this day forward, my prayers became colloquial. No longer imploring, I questioned and asked: "Is this Your answer to last night's prayer?" "Is death what You think I can handle?" I wanted to scream as loud as I could, but I only had the strength to mentally whisper: "Dear Lord, really?" "How could this happen to us?" Never in my life had I felt so close to giving up or understanding the feeling of defeat. The word widow did not even enter my mind. I could only think of Randy in terms of his death and not my widowhood.

In Latin America, New Year's Eve is a time of big partying, with more festivities than Christmas because there is no solemnity—only the celebration putting the past behind us or anticipating the fulfillment of what is to be. If we traveled to Panama for the holidays, we would convene at my cousin's home which would be overflowing with food, music, and dancing. At the turn of the year, we always ate 12 grapes (one for each month) for good fortune. The times when we remained in the United States, I still liked to have some sort of celebration on December 31st. However, this holiday was forever changed for our family.

I suppose I must have nodded off at some point that night, but it could not have been for more than a few hours. Anxiety had set in and my heart was either bursting out of my chest or not beating at all. In facing our past crises, I had ample experience with mental anguish and fear, but I had never felt the physical manifestations of anxiety. This was different. I, who had never felt clinical anxiety, was having panic attacks. Remembering to breathe became a thing. Over the next few days I would gasp for air and fill my lungs to capacity because in between those moments, I found myself forgetting to inhale.

My eyes were so swollen that I became physically unable to cry because my tear ducts were completely obstructed. The sadness and despair were beyond anything I had ever felt, and they were always present. I was stunned by what had happened—that our lives had become a full flung tragedy, and that I was worthy of being pitied. In between the sadness and despair I had flashes of anger because I realized that I was the one left holding the bag, while Randy was in "peace." Anger made me feel alive, but it was fleeting, and it subsided quickly— immediately being replaced by anxiety. I questioned how I would raise three boys, make a living and handle a home without Randy at my side. I could not hold thoughts about the future for more than a few seconds because the grief was so overwhelming that it quickly overcame and enveloped me.

I don't remember eating, dressing, or even seeing my children. In the solitude of my bedroom, I would claw at the air, grasping at the empty space or desperately holding onto my pillow as if it were the only thing preventing me from sinking into the immeasurable depths of my despondency. There was no relief from the hurt that engulfed my soul except when I tried to communicate with Randy. Speaking my feelings was not comforting but writing felt good. My letters allowed me to express the suffering that never abandoned me, that consoled me in ways that are hard to explain and allowed me to consider thoughts I dared not say out loud.

January 1, 2010 (Day 2)

Dear Randy,

I miss you so, so much. It is so painful to think of you, but I cherish your smell which still lingers on your clothes.

It hurts so bad to realize that I'll never hear you say, "Hi beautiful" ever again. And I won't have your opinion anymore. And it hurts my heart that we will never hold hands again. What I would not give for a brief moment with you to tell you that I love you very much.

I. Love. You.

I wish I had said this more in your last month. I love the husband that you became and the father that you learned to be. I love your goodness, your gentleness, your selflessness, and all that the boys and I are to you. I will cherish you and I will make sure that the boys treasure your memory.

I've zip locked your shirts that hold your scent. I love smelling you: it is the closest I can get to you now. I hope you are feeling my love and that you have taken it with you.

Because of the holiday season, my parents and my brother were visiting. I suppose everyone was busy lending a helping hand. My godfather came over to fix a bathroom and asked my dad for a short shovel which must have been in the garage. Dad was very tidy and organized. However, the garage was not. It was Randy's domain and being an artist, tidiness was not his strong suit. Plus, he had a photographic memory, so things did not have to be orderly for him to find them.

My father was aware of our inordinately messy garage and he thought it would be unlikely to ever find anything there. Somehow, his eyes fell on the right place to retrieve the tool. A while later, my uncle made another request, this time for a chisel. My father thought it would be impossible to repeat the luck of the first time but again, he achieved a small victory immediately, finding the chisel. Both men remarked that Randy must be overseeing them fixing the bathroom toilet.

Randy was a very handy man—more than most men unless they are in the trade. He loved to work with his hands, especially on wood. Nothing gave him more pleasure than to sand and varnish the teak rails on our boat. "Deb, most people hate boat maintenance, but I love to work on Blue Chip on a sunny and crisp California day." In addition to having the talent to make things look visually beautiful on film, he was also capable of building his visions which translated into props and photography sets, bathrooms, and decks for our house. He could construct or fix anything. If there are handymen in heaven, Randy would want to be a carpenter.

In every battle we faced before, we were always optimistic, believing we would prevail over all the adversity life had hurled at us. Randy was hugely positive, and I was grounded in realism, but we always felt that together we would win and come out at the other end. It was only after the trials of the last year that we had started to feel the possibility of defeat, but even then, we always hoped for the best. Suddenly, the rug was pulled out from under both of us. He was gone, and I was alone dealing with the life altering concept of "Never." In the twinkling of an eye he was out of the fight and the silence left by his absence was deafening.

Our background was incredibly different, but our love transcended distance, culture, race, language, borders, and all that should have separated us. Ultimately, it made us stronger. We were seasoned warriors.

I lost my soul mate and the absoluteness of NEVER had started to sink in. I could not fathom my new reality and the thought of it was taking me down into a deep abyss. I would come out gasping for air and once again, sink into the mire of my anguished thoughts.

Randy's multiple visits to the ER, his hospitalizations and the rehabs had turned me into an expert crisis manager. These episodes hurled me into the vortex of the unexpected and awakened the most existential fears I could ever imagine. I thought I had visited breakpoint many times, but his death proved me sorrowfully wrong. I had never experienced anything like this crushing maverick of a wave. Nothing could compare to the heartache, fear and sadness that permeated every single cell of my body. Even the marrow of my bones felt this loss and tearing out my hair would have brought relief because it would have been one less thing that hurt. What was worse, no one in my circle could even begin to comprehend, much less relate, to my bereavement. I felt very alone.

January 2, 2010 (Day 3)

Dear Randy,

I just keep waiting to wake up from a bad dream. Each day I expect you to come back from a trip. The most painful thing is the concept of never. Never will we work together again. Never will you photograph the boys. Never will you drive your Porsche. Never will you give me an opinion. It is so final and that is so intensely hurtful.

I miss you so much and I wish I could hug you or just hold your hand. The boys are grieving for you as well. David feels like a little man. He is processing the grief and he cries loud and hard when it strikes him. I told him that we will never get past it, but that we will learn to live with this sadness. He utters the phrase, "that's a secret my Dad took with him" when he does not know the answer to a question of something that pertains to you.

Michael is the thinker and he wants to know how this will affect him. He wanted to claim your things and he asked me if I'll ever get married again. I know he is sad inside, but he does not cry or talk about it.

Christian is blessedly unaware, but I feel so much sadness for him because he will not know you. You were such a hands-on father and did so, so much with the boys. Christian does talk about you and loves you in his own little way. He thinks you are away on a trip.

I finally had a talk with the older boys. They were hurt and confused. Their faces immediately brightened up when I said: "Daddy is in Heaven, with Jesus." I was thankful for the solid faith formation they received at St. Paul because they did not need explanations to understand the peace and promise of that notion. As they heard that "Daddy is not hurting anymore" I could see their relief, even though they were still so very sad. When I added, "Don't worry, Jesus will take care of us" it allayed some of their fears.

I was certain Randy's own demise would have caught him by surprise. He had a PhD in his capacity to deny the inevitability of death. His incredible filter was mostly a positive attribute but also a fatal flaw because it kept him from inventorying his health. In the 20 plus years I had known him, only once had he ever considered his own end. We were young enough to treat it as a joke "Death and taxes are the only certainty in life" but even then, he would smile and let me ramble on while he remained silent. To Randy, dying was a foreign topic that did not pertain to his existence. In fact, he was supposed to be my caretaker in the sunset of our lives . . . and I'd go first. But the timing was reversed, and we had never contemplated this scenario in our script. Life had dealt out the wrong cards. Randy was out, and somehow, I still remained in the game.

I realized the blessing to be alive and to have my parents, my brother and wonderful friends surrounding me. I knew they would help me put together this puzzle my life had become. A new set of pieces had been thrown into the box while others were forever lost. I could not visualize what the new picture would look like but even in the midst of my despondency, I was grateful for the support system that enveloped me. Nevertheless, pangs of guilt assaulted me because I was alive and Randy was not. Yet I did not want to face what lay ahead of me. I wanted to trade places.

Once the coroner released Randy's remains, I was finally able to set a date for the funeral service. The cause of death would not be forthcoming for several weeks, so my questions remained unanswered. What caused this? Was it his kidneys? Had the doctors overlooked something? I could have driven myself crazy trying to conjure up an explanation, but my mind had already run out of steam. Instead, I chose to center on his funeral. "When I go, I want to be cremated" I used to joke with Randy, making him know what I wanted because I thought he would outlive me. I knew he would approve.

His service became the focus of my existence. I wanted it to be glorious, a celebration of my husband and of his life. He probably would not have wanted me to fuss over this because he was so low key and preferred small groups. When he turned 40, Randy went to a Formula 1 race in Montreal with his buddies. When I turned 40, Amy and I threw ourselves a big birthday bash. His artistic nature thrived on the feelings elicited by his work and he loved when his photographs were admired and recognized, but Randy never self-promoted.

January 4 (Day 5)

Dear Randy,

I will never be loved as much again. I am mourning the loss of your love which was so, so, much. No one will ever love me again like you.

Amy felt you last night. She woke up drenched in sweat but feeling very calm. You both were on Blue Chip and you were wearing a dark fleece, handling some kind of teak device that was the color of the sky or like moving water. She said that you were very calm but indicated that she should watch out for me on your behalf. You were worried about me but not in an anxious way. The feeling is that you were away on some trip, but we would be together again. There was the smell of coffee in the air.

I'm planning your funeral service and this keeps me serene. It does not hurt so bad today, although I did not sleep for more than three hours. Somehow, I'm getting through the day. I love you tonight.

Christian was happy to be in your closet tonight and to touch your clothes. I showed him your picture and he said with a smile, "Daddy does not have an owie." We kissed and kissed you. Did you feel that? I'm trying to preserve your memory for the boys. I was thinking of putting your ashes in one of the Oaxaca black vases. Wouldn't that be perfect? I'm not so sure of the mausoleum niche. It's rather expensive and did not feel right. I was thinking of keeping you here at home, so we could light a candle on special days and remember you.

My mom, my brother and the two older boys left on the cruise. We decided this trip would be a distraction since the funeral could not be held until the following week. I could barely put one foot in front of the other and I had not left the house since the night we returned from the ER. The idea of getting on a cruise ship and having to be present was jarring. I also wanted the older boys to have a break from all of the emotion and sadness that seeped out from every one of my pores. I needed to remain in the sanctuary of our home, so Christian and I did not travel. My father also stayed back for company and to watch over us. Functioning on fumes, I pulled myself together to do the minimum necessary to manage life and more importantly, to plan Randy's funeral.

I was assaulted by the surprising sensation of respite. After being dragged into the depths of darkness, I was caught off guard by the sudden feeling of nothing. Could it be that my grieving had stopped? Was my suffering over? After days of crying I was suddenly unable to shed a tear and my eyes started to look somewhat normal (only slightly puffy). I wondered if perhaps I was done being sad. My despair had abated into numbness and my grief had gone into remission. I felt guilty for not being sad but welcomed the respite because everything from my soul to my entrails ached. In the mere five days since Randy's death, my existence was morphing into a new reality, whether I accepted it or not. In doing so, the core and shell of my being molted . . . the longing and pain were indescribable. I was briefly anesthetized, and every fiber of my being embraced the nothingness. Later I would learn that this interlude was normal, it was just the body, soul and mind needing time to recover. The awful grief would return.

I was surprised how so many people asked if I was taking meds. Are. You. Kidding? After all that I went through with Randy? "I hate meds and the medical community who prescribes them" I thought disparagingly as I brushed off the question or answered candidly, "No, I'm not taking medication, why would I?" If I had the strength to be furious, I would have been livid with the doctors, the pills, and modern medicine. Instead, I could only muster the indignation to be disgusted. To me it was all a big failure that blindsided Randy and destroyed my life. "If I ever succumb to the meds, it will be a last case scenario which I'll do kicking and screaming."

Being despondent, sad, or anxious was entirely normal and these feelings needed to be respected and honored. I chose to feel this aspect of my humanity, not because I wanted to experience pain but dulling it with medications was not a solution I wanted to use. If there was ever a time to wallow in misery, this was it. I could fully relate to the notion of tearing out my hair or covering myself in a black shroud. I was slowly sinking into the quagmire and all I could do was come up for air right before I choked. I considered myself a strong woman, but the defeated warrior in me entertained the notion of fading away and dying. Departing this miserable life sounded like a relief, but I had 3 little boys who needed me. I was not a single parent; I was all they had left. While I had no desire to be tortured by the unrelenting and agonizing feelings, living was necessary, and the meds were unacceptable. Grief was the price I paid for loving.

Lack of sleep was definitely a concern. I was only getting about an hour or so a day which was becoming just as debilitating as the sadness and fear that enveloped me. I went to Dr. Chong for acupuncture. She was the real deal: Chinese, medically trained at a top university and a practitioner of traditional Chinese medicine for decades. I found her when Randy needed help for his back pain and anxiety. She had no inkling of his death but just one look at my face, my tongue and my pulses were all she needed to declare: "You are a mess." No kidding. She treated me and that night I slept for 4 hours, the next day I clocked 5 hours and finally, 7 hours.

January 5 (Day 6)

Dear Randy,

Yesterday was a good day. I met with Father Guy who counseled and confessed me. We planned your mass. I want it to be a beautiful celebration of you. I'm thankful to be in his spiritual hands. He is a wonderful priest.

I had a great conversation with the funeral coordinator. She affirmed your visit to Amy. Even though I'd love a visit from you, I know I'm not ready because I would not be able to fully experience you and relish that moment. But you came to my best friend and you were in your version of a peaceful place. I also understand why you came to my Dad. You are coming to those who are important to me.

I also met with Dr. Krempler (the school principal) and it was also a great visit. For now, we don't have to worry about tuition. We are in such a good place. I told him how you were the quiet force behind my volunteering. In particular, the President thing. Thank you for encouraging that and for all you provided: the time, the money, the lifestyle, the babysitting, the physical help, and the opinion. Again, those are the things I will miss.

Finally, I also met up with Debbie S. She shared that she too was a widow which I did not know. When I confessed my numbness and thought I was not sad anymore, she explained that numb is OK. It's just a reprieve so I can carry on. That the sadness will come again but for now, I'm getting a little break. Last night I slept for 7 hours.

The funeral coordinator was also a widow, albeit much older than me. "Look out for the dreams, that is when they come to visit us." Her comment lent further credence to what I had been told about our loved ones coming back to check on us and I remarked "I can hardly wait for my visit!"

My best friend, Amy, accompanied me to the funeral coordination meeting. She was a big part of our lives and was there to support and plan for Randy's memorial. Amy and I were bonded by children, volunteering, and a copious amount of personal drama. Moreover, we were chronologically aligned by being born, married and giving birth practically at the same time (or within mere months of each other). She was capable of lighting up a room with her presence, but she also knew how to be a tiny glow by my side, so the darkness did not overwhelm me.

Amy overhead my remark to the funeral coordinator, "I can hardly wait for Randy's visit." As we left the church office, she observed me carefully and said softly: "Deb, I did not share this with you because I did not know how you would take it . . . if you would be ready to hear this . . . but after your conversation with that lady, I think this is the right time. Randy came to see me last night."

She recounted her dream, his visit. All of Randy's "elements" were an integral part of her experience: our boat, the teak, the smell of coffee. Ever since he was of age, Randy had always owned boats and he derived great pleasure from fixing and puttering over them. He delighted in the look, feel and care of the teak on Blue Chip, our Grand Banks 32'. His perfect day was varnishing the teak wood rails and trimmings, on a sunny California morning, and nursing a cup of freshly brewed coffee. When Amy described her dream, it was my gift for the day. I was able to imagine what Randy's heaven would look like and it was so fitting. She also saw him looking restored, at peace and ready as if heading out on a long journey.

Amy's experience held my rapt attention. I hung on to each and every word. She called it a dream because she was asleep, but it was more vivid and real than any dream she had ever known. She awoke drenched in perspiration, but with a calmness and peace that permeated her body. It was an experience like she had never had in her life and I relished her dream. We analyzed each element and it was poignant. The notion that Randy was going to travel far away was laden with familiarity and I could cling to the visual of him departing to an unknown destination.

The summer Christian was born, my parents took David and Michael to Panama, so I could have a little break. It was sheer bliss to devote two entire months to a new baby while having the maturity and confidence of being a practiced mother. We took advantage of this generous gift of time by going out to California and cruising the open ocean on Blue Chip. We went from Newport to Catalina, through the Channel Islands and finally to Santa Barbara. Crossing those unprotected waters was one of Randy's big life dreams. It should have been scary to me, but he was a practiced sailor and I was consumed with Christian. I did not give a second thought about venturing into the open ocean because I trusted Randy's abilities and prudence. Amy's dream reminded me of my husband's planning for the unknown, anticipating the challenge and his quiet excitement of undertaking a new project. It was soothing to think of him at the helm of our boat with his eyes squinting on the horizon, scanning the blue vastness of the Pacific Ocean.

My visit with Dr. Krempler, the school principal, was another moment that infused my troubled soul with peace. During my years at the PTA, he and I had been involved in many moments of unfortunate drama as sometimes can happen when women, personalities, and egos are not aligned with the common goal of serving the school. Dr. Krempler knew me well and was fond of our family, so this was a hard visit for him as well. He disclosed that an anonymous angel had covered the tuition for David and Michael for the rest of the year and that financial assistance would be available as we moved forward. I could not help but remember Randy's observation that "After all of the hours you give and the funds you've raised for St. Paul, we should get a designated parking space . . . or some free tuition" I used to laugh and brush off his comments, never imagining that I would be on the receiving end.

Both Amy's revelation and the principal's assurances were blessings that eased my pain, comforted my concerns and answered my prayers in the midst of this tragedy. I was in awe of how our family's needs were met, including an education fund set up by Lisa, my successor on the PTA Board.

> *January 6 (Day 7)*
>
> *Dear Randy,*
>
> *Today is one week.*
>
> *I am reflecting on your life and your achievements . . . I feel so fortunate to have been part of it all. To have been your choice, to have experienced your amazing career and talent. What a life you gave me, with highs and with lows of such magnitude that I was forced to come to this spiritual place which now blesses me.*
>
> *You are no ordinary man. When looking at your body of work, I am still amazed at your talent. World class. I took all of what you achieved for granted, or rather, I felt I was entitled given my own accomplishments. But I want to tell you that it was awesome, that I was privileged, that I was blessed you came into my life and that you've given me enough memories to humble me but also to carry on.*

Today was hard. It was the first time I was truly alone in the house. Once I was certain Dad and Christian were gone, I locked myself in our bedroom. I started to feel so sad about not telling you that I loved you in the last few weeks. I know I must forgive myself for that one. Were you around when I started to break down? It was as if you're OK letting me cry about everything else but not that particular regret . . . because you know how much I did love you.

The house was empty but the sound of footsteps and loudly clicking light switches halted the beginning of my personal pity party. The noise sounded just like when you used to walk around turning off the lights and saying that the house was "lit up like a Christmas tree."

The noise was such that it interrupted my crying session which I had just barely started. I left our room and walked to the garage to see if Dad had come back but no one else was at home. I then returned to resume my pity party and at that very moment, Amy called. She was here in less than three minutes. It was as though you were not going to let me get hung up on that regret, and so you instigated her phone call.

Frances arrived in the afternoon while Lee-Anne and I were going over your eulogy. I want it to be beautiful for you and a treasured memory for the boys. She was the perfect choice to write this. I had a great "girls night out" with Lisa K, Susan B, Shari and Frances. Such wonderful girlfriends. Lisa set up an education fund for the boys.

Jorge A. called last night, and we had a great conversation. I did not cry before falling asleep. It was a day of many little gifts that somehow eased my sadness, pain, and anxiety.

Regrets. Nothing approximates the finality of death: there are no second chances for thoughts unsaid, feelings suppressed, or intentions to share. There was one lament that weighed heavily on my heart. I had not verbally conveyed my love to Randy during his last month of life. I was the proverbial "don't tell me, do for me." To me, actions spoke louder than words, but Randy felt loved when he heard it, when he was told. He was not a needy man, yet I knew I should have said, "I love you" more frequently and meaningfully in the past weeks. Neither did I hold his hands during all of the times we were together in the hospital. I was so wrapped up in my own thoughts of dealing and managing our situation that I was not fully present when I visited. Never did it cross my mind that I would not have another chance. My heart ached with contrition. This self-condemnation would have consumed me had I not experienced the interruption of my pity party—twice: first with the clanking sounds in my empty home and second, with Amy's phone call. I took this to mean that Randy did not want me to dwell in anguish because he knew beyond measure that I loved him.

Because of the emails I had sent the previous month, a few of my friends from Latin America were aware of our family's situation. I had remained close to my Mexican posse throughout the years and the bonds of those friendships were tight. One of my classmates offered a glimmer of hope that permeated every fiber of my being. As an engineer, my thinking tended to be linear. But Claudia offered a tantalizing alternative. "Debbie, what if time in Heaven is non-linear?" "What if Heaven is not bound by our earthly concept of time, space and matter?" My technical mind attempted but could not grasp the astrophysical implications of such concepts except for one fact that mattered to me. If this were the case, then I could still tell Randy I loved him. Somehow, he would receive my words now and feel them. I clung onto this possibility because it soothed my tattered psyche.

January 7th (Day 8) - Friday

Dear Randy,

Once again, I'm crying a lot for you. The sadness is back replacing the numbness, but it is OK because crying releases these bottled up feelings. I was out today preparing for your funeral mass. Dad and Frances brought your ashes home, in the Oaxaca vase, which will now serve as your urn. What a perfect place for you.

Lee Anne polished up your eulogy. I hope it celebrates you, is a fitting memorial and shapes your legacy to the boys. I feel like you are away on some trip and you will soon be back. When I realize I won't see you again, the sadness takes over.

Lee Anne was a mom friend who headed up the Cub Scout program at St. Paul. Her youngest son was Michael's classmate, but she had two boys who were much older, so we looked up to her for guidance and advice. She effectively mobilized the fathers to volunteer and was also my manager for the fashion line, so we spent a lot of time together and she knew Randy more than most in my circle. Lee Anne was a gifted writer and I turned to her for help in composing Randy's eulogy. She was eloquent but measured, thoughtfully elegant and strategic, simply perfect for this task. It was my mission to make this a glorious celebration because I felt that somehow, Randy would see it or hear it. It was my goodbye to him.

"Deb, think of the many that have never experienced love as you have. At least you know what it is to be truly and fully loved." At the moment, LeeAnne's words did not ease my pain but I tucked them away in the far corners of my mind. Later, I would open this box when I was ready to be comforted by her pearls of wisdom.

January 8th (Day 9) - Saturday

Dear Randy,

Seven hours last night. I was so tired I did not cry myself to sleep and I woke up rested.

I had a "moment" this morning when Christian wanted to sit at the table instead of in his highchair. I remembered your remark when we first brought him home from the hospital. As you looked at our kitchen table for four, you said "All I want to know is how we are going to fit 5 people here." Now we don't have to think about that. This sucks.

Christian was our trophy baby. When I was a little girl, I would always say I wanted to have three kids, perhaps because I only had one other sibling. I also wanted to have my last pregnancy before I hit 40. When the older boys were toddlers, I held off from having a third child since our marriage was in shambles, but as things got better, we took the plunge. Two months shy of my big birthday, I delivered a gorgeous baby boy who was six years and eight years younger than Michael and David, respectively.

Christian signified that we had worked through it all and had come out on the other end of the tunnel. This child was pure delight and he was constantly at our side. By then, we had the experience, the patience, and the perspective of being practiced parents. I devoted time to this baby in ways that were not possible when the first two were little. Randy and I used to cart him all around town as we worked together on photo shoots or went through our daily routine. We would joke and say we were going to spoil this baby rotten, forget about any discipline, and just set up a trust fund for his future so we could totally enjoy him without a care in the world.

This little person, in his innocence and oblivion, was my oasis in the arid dessert of my despondency. His spirit had no knowledge of our loss, so he was my great escape from what weighed on the rest of the family. Here was a soul that was pure joy, a bright light in my life, and my source of immeasurable comfort. Even though he was a boy, Christian was often described as beautiful by strangers who stopped to admire his wide dark eyes, creamy white skin, and his rosebud mouth that was framed by a perfect head of dark hair. He was the proverbial "easy" child: cheerful, adaptable and effortless. I grieved the father he loved in his own little way and whom he would never get to know. It was hard to accept that eventually, Christian would forget Randy while the other two boys had complicated paths ahead.

January 11 (Day 12) - Monday

Dear Randy,

The boys came back from the cruise yesterday. Going away was a good distraction for them and I needed this break to process my many new feelings. David is very much mourning you and saddened by all that he knows . . . he will miss the time with you and the wonderful father that you were.

David dreamt of you the day after he went snorkeling. You were both varnishing the rails on Blue Chip, and I was in the cabin making coffee. You were wearing your blue painting shorts and the red flag Reyn Spooner shirt. He woke up from his dream feeling very happy. I explained to David that this dream was like a visit and that it was a little gift for both of us.

Michael is grieving in a much more complex way. Silently. It is coming out in his behavior and I guess, in sleep. I am helping him by asking him to verbalize his thoughts and then I try to explain them to him.

Your parents arrived yesterday. That is tough on me. It is painful to see your mom and I find it hard to offer them comfort, but I'm trying my best. Duwayne also came in from Hawaii yesterday. So great to see him and have him remember you from that time of our lives. He really got to experience your humor and how funny you could be in an understated way. He thinks you are the funniest person he ever met.

Duwayne was Randy's best man at our wedding. They met at Brooks and bonded over class assignments, compatible personalities and good humor. The first time he ever traveled outside of the US was for our wedding in Panama. Being half Chinese and half Japanese, he blended seamlessly with my side of the family, looking far more in place than Randy, the only white guy. So many shared memories . . . It was such a comfort to have him be with me. Frances, Christian's godmother, was also a source of strength. She also loved Randy and knew him from the beginning of "us"—when we were just a young couple. Jorge, Michael's godfather, also would be arriving from Panama. To his regret, he did not make it to our wedding, but he was coming to lend his support at this ceremony that marked my next life-altering event. I treasured my afar friends, those who knew us as individuals and later as a couple. My current world knew me simply as a mom and a parent, but these were lifelong friends that had journeyed with both of us and they added a whole other reality to my situation. They were present, having crossed oceans to say goodbye to Randy and offer their support to me.

The Funeral

January 12 (Day 13) - Tuesday

*Jorge and Pete arrived today. This is the big day I have
been focused on and planning. I was so nervous going to
the church. If there was ever a moment I thought I'd need a
tranquilizer, this was it.*

*I wore the ETCETERA winter white skirt that you thought was
so cool. My first choice was the Orla Keeley dress that you
bought me in London, but the weather was record low. The
days leading up to your funeral mass were so, so cold. The
boys wore their best dress jackets and Christian looked so
cute in his sailor suit. They carried the gifts to the altar, and I
was told watching the three of them walk up was touching and
poignant. The older ones left Christian to make his way back
on his own to the pews. Poor little baby, he has no idea what
is going on. David cried his heart out from beginning to end.
He is being so straightforward with his mourning. Michael did
not shed a tear. He was just quiet and stoic.*

*It was a beautiful mass and I tried to make it a fitting tribute to
you. I am so thankful to Amy and the girls for allowing me to
focus just on that, so it could be graceful and memorable. They
took care of the reception which I hear was very lovely. I never
got past our kitchen—the house has never been so crowded.
So many people came here to honor you and us. It must have
been over 300. I have no idea, but the church was full.*

*It was important to our families, our boys and me that you were
properly honored. I wanted everyone to see what you had
become and what you had achieved. I did a photo montage*

147

of your work—my favorite photos. They provided a beautiful imagery of how you saw the world, the way it ought to be. I want the boys to be proud of you. Pete delivered your eulogy in a very touching way. It was all very emotional for everyone who attended. There were very few dry eyes in the pews.

I was terribly nervous heading out to the service, butterflies flitted in my gut and my hands trembled. For the first time since Randy's death I would be surrounded by so many people and I did not want to fall apart. The funeral mass was my tribute to Randy, intended to be a beautiful celebration of his life. Duwayne's thoughts were, "Deb, you did great, but I don't think so much pomp was Randy's style. He was way low key." I wanted it to be the best that I could possibly prepare, so I paid attention to every detail and was vested in all that mattered. I had chaired many fundraisers and galas, but never again would I apply my skills to such a personal purpose. At some subconscious level, I must have also understood that I was leaving behind my life as a volunteer and event planner. I had no idea how difficult moving forward was going to be, but I knew that I was on a journey with no return. Randy's funeral was also my way of saying goodbye to life as I had known it.

My own wedding had not mattered much to me. I did not even choose the cake, the venue nor any of the particulars. Having married in Panama, all we had to do was show up with my dress and his tuxedo because my parents took care of the rest. Randy's family was in California, so Florida was the middle ground. At first, we thought we could do the planning ourselves. After two weekends of trying to find the perfect venue and contemplating all of the logistics that were involved, Randy gave up and said, "Deb, let your mom do it for us."

For Randy's funeral, I orchestrated every single detail, each song, every reading. Amy did the flower arrangements and they were artistic, remarkable, and non-traditional. The music was moving, and his eulogy was touching. Pete, his producer and close colleague, flew in from California to deliver it. It was heartfelt and moving. I put together a video of Randy's most iconic photos, many of which included our friends and their children as models. When his portfolio popped up on the church's mega screen, Randy came alive through the impact of his images. They were spectacular and breathtaking. There were few dry eyes, but I held my composure in an Oscar worthy performance. Everyone thought I was so strong, but my tears were momentarily under control. From here onward they would be shed in solace of my room or the privacy of my shower. I cried every night, once the day was over when no one could see me—especially my sons who would not benefit from a crumbling mother.

Later, our home was packed with well-wishers, cars were lined up and down our street, and children were running in and out. I don't remember much except parking myself in a corner by the kitchen and the sudden departure of some friends. An earthquake happened in Haiti and they had family on the island. Later I would learn about the devastation and tragedy that followed. I was able to relate to this earth-shattering experience in a more profound way than I had ever imagined possible because I myself was bogged down in my own morass.

Despite their most heartfelt intentions, few people were really able to offer a meaningful condolence. No words could assuage my pain, but thankfully I was mostly spared from the insensitive except for an occasion or two. The best condolence I received was a tight hug, an expressive eye connection, and the sharing of a common moment of empathy. No need for words or advice.

With Randy's funeral behind me I closed the shortest yet the darkest chapter in my life. Just as I became a wife at our wedding, Randy's funeral marked my new status as a widow. I still had to come to terms with that notion which conjured up images of a shrouded in black, bent over, and gnarled old woman. Somehow, she and I shared this unwanted stigma.

Ahead of me lay the terrifying and daunting task of figuring out what came next and how I would chart my future course. I had no direction and lacked the energy to put one foot in front of the next. I had rallied for the funeral because it gave me purpose. I poured out my everything to honor Randy and I stayed strong until it was over. But the service sapped whatever little was left in me. As I laid down and sank into my pillow crying, all I wanted to do was pull the bedcovers over my head and never crawl out of bed again.

Why?

"But who are you, a human being, to talk back to God?
Shall what is formed say to the one who formed it,
'Why did you make me like this?'"

Romans 9:20

January 15 (Day 16) - Friday

Dear Randy,

I'm thankful your parents have left, especially your mom. The grief of losing a son is unimaginable to me. However, we are on different planes and I can't relate to them. There is nothing left inside of me, nothing I can do for her, and it's just painful to be around your parents.

I was relieved that my in-laws were returning to California. With the funeral behind me, I had to resume some semblance of life, even though I barely had the stamina to get out of bed. Anything depleting made me wince and Randy's family was too much to bear. I still had to breathe my way out of the panic attacks. The bills and paperwork were piling up and they needed my attention. I had not come to terms with my new identity as a widow, but the legality of my new status could not wait for my acknowledgment. It was happening whether I wanted it to or not.

> *January 17 (Day 18) - Sunday*
>
> *Dear Randy,*
>
> *This morning I woke up with more, if possible, than the usual sadness. I had flashes of our special moments: the apartment in Houston, the cabin in Big Bear, the hot springs on the road to Mammoth, visiting Mono Lake . . . then when I was fully awake, the grief overtook me. These were such old and special memories that came to me as I was in a state of semi-awareness: not asleep but not awake. They showed up like rapidly flashing PowerPoint slides in front of me. Susan told me that it was my unconscious mind dealing with all of this and that I had to allow and feel the process. Ever since then, I have not awakened in tears.*

When I "saw" all those old and uniquely special memories, I was shaken and confused. It was surreal how they popped up as I was emerging from my dream state— even before it was daylight. I panicked and felt overwhelmed. I thought I was on the verge of losing my mind. Who could explain what was happening to me? I immediately called Susan, the counselor who saved our marriage.

- "Susan, what in the world was that?"

- "It's your subconscious processing your loss. Let the grief flow," she explained.

- "But Susan, this really hurts and it's scary. I think I'm going crazy."

- "I know honey, but you should not suppress it. It has to come out. If not now, it will show up later in very inappropriate ways."

Having always trusted Susan, I took her advice to heart. I was not ready to grab onto the handlebars of my life, but I did not want to be further handicapped by strange behavior, memory loss or misplaced anger when the moment came to cast off my training wheels and steer my unicycle. If I buried my emotions, they might resurrect with rage and rear up in the most unsuitable moments or improper ways. No one wants to experience the bruising pain of grief, but I had to feel it in order to heal. It was like opening a festering wound for cleaning and redressing. It had to be done. Otherwise, my heart could not mend. Choosing to feel was the lesser of two evils if I wanted to come out of this a stronger woman.

After missing classes for almost two weeks, David and Michael returned to school. I was still unable to drive because my nerves were shot and my reflexes were gone. In both a literal and practical sense, I was not ready to sit behind a steering wheel without being a hazard to myself and other drivers. Thankfully, my parents were still around to help. At best, my emotional state was fragile and the simplest of tasks seemed like an insurmountable challenge.

I finally received Randy's death certificate. It read, "Acute Myocardial Infarction." In other words, a heart attack. I read this over and over, but it did not register. Of all the problems we faced (as well as what the hospital had evaluated), this was the one issue that had never been mentioned. I was so incredulous that I found the strength to contact the coroner. When I finally managed to talk to a live person, I was told to call back in three weeks because some lab results were still pending.

A heart attack. Even though I had no idea what to expect, this made no sense to me. What would cause heart failure? An obstruction? A weakness? Medication? I had no idea. Once more I found myself in the familiar situation of having more questions than answers. By then, life

153

had given me ample practice in dealing with the unknown, so I could put the questions aside and wait for the eventual explanation.

January 20 (Three weeks) - Wednesday

Dear Randy,

The Grief and the Worries are so much. I can barely function. I miss you and our love terribly. The emptiness is so vast and overwhelming. I wish it was a year later because it cannot possibly be this hard by then. My heart hurts so intensely. Even though I try to rationalize what it would have been like had you recovered partially, these thoughts do not bring comfort because my strongest memories of you are when you were whole, healthy and my true better half.

Jan 21 – Thursday

Dear Randy,

I have been thinking a lot about your hands. They were so strong, blunt, and caring. I miss your hands. Last night I had a dream:

"I was outdoors, under a shelter, sitting on a picnic table. Suddenly, you were there, and I was surprised. I sat next to you and said, "I get to hold your hands again." And I held them. They were so warm and tangible."

I was so happy when I woke up feeling that I had touched Randy's hands again. The pain and suffering that inhabited me had become so familiar that feeling peace and joy took me by surprise. These feelings did not last long. A few moments later, as I tried to tackle some paperwork, I realized that Blue Chip's insurance had been terminated. Having to deal with boat problems immediately put me in a bad place and my frayed nerves started to quaver again. A simple task that an earlier version of me would have glossed over caused my whole body to fall apart. I went into a paralyzing depression. The sadness was so intense that I could not move. I felt incredibly tired and incapable of going on. I retreated into my bedroom, wanting to close the door to the world.

Thankfully, my friend, Adrine, was on her way to me that morning. We had thrown a bridal shower and baby showers for each other. We shared a special bond because our families knew each other from the Venezuela days. Our husbands had also enjoyed each other's company. She nudged me out of my despondency for the moment. "Debbie, Randy was meant to have a short life. That's why he lived so fully and accomplished so much." To Adrine, it all fell into place: "Girl, Randy was such a good person he did not need a priest to give him last rites or hear his confession. He learned all he needed to on this earth, and he grew spiritually as a man, husband, and father." Her words took me back to September, when Randy acknowledged that he would be content with a simplified life. That month was so perfect, and I found comfort remembering Randy's spiritual and emotional summit.

She also shared that a few years ago, her father had narrowly escaped a life-threatening health complication. He had seen a tunnel of light, but he was unable to step into it. Her dad was still alive, but her mom was not. Adrine was with her when she died. "I saw a light in her eyes right before she finally closed them." I hoped Randy had the same peace when he passed. My last memory of him consoled me: waking up and seeing how rested and peaceful he looked.

A second conversation with a cousin, who had lost her mom as a little girl, assured me she had felt her mother's love in wonderful and miraculous ways. "On my wedding day as we were driving to the chapel, I stopped by my mom's grave. Just as the car pulled up, I heard my mom's favorite song on the radio, and I knew she was with me." It was an unusual occurrence because the song was old and not in the station's usual playlist. My cousin was certain that my boys would have similar experiences of their own. As I witnessed the void in David's life—missing his father—I found comfort in the notion that each of us would continue to have our relationship with him in our own way. David was very upset at not being able to say goodbye to Randy. "I am not going to lead a normal life" he cried. "I wish I had not been born into this cursed family." Michael, who was eight, showed his grief in other ways, like having a hard time falling asleep, restless nights or simply, missing Randy's presence and acting out. I knew that they had to remember their dad and it was up to me to keep his memory alive.

The pendulum between knowing Randy had died and accepting my widowhood was constantly swinging. His death was easier to accept if I imagined that he was healthy, on a far-away trip. Such musings erased the notion of "never" and "forever" because our connection could not be severed, and I would meet up with him eventually. His visits in my dreams brought me comfort. My widowhood still did not feel real.

Jan 24 – Sunday

Dear Randy,

I dreamt of us again:

"We were at a hotel in Europe. You were explaining to me how they would give you your pill in a little grey box at the hospital but somehow, it was not the hospital but our bedroom. You also told me that your assistant always made sure you had your pill, even when you were supposed to be healthy. She would hide it under your placemat.

Then, I looked into your eyes and you were crying. Two large tears slipped down your face and somehow you conveyed that you were sorry it had to be like this, that you were not really better but still addicted. You were so sad about this. We held hands."

I feel that you are worried about me. I feel you are sorry that things did not turn out the way we dreamt they would. But I also want you to know that I'm grateful for the times that were good and that I'm aware of how it pained you to struggle and put me through all that you did. I realize how very strong you really were, and I don't need to know that you are sorry. I forgive you.

I immediately journaled this dream when I woke up. It was full of symbolism and laden with feelings that were confusing, yet I had no doubt it was a unique experience. To "see" Randy's tears pierced my soul. In this dream, Randy was conveying addiction and sadness yet, his cause of death was a heart attack. I could not reconcile one with the other, but the experience was unforgettable and meaningful.

Jan 25 – Monday

Dear Randy,

David wants to know what caused your heart attack. He also wants to know if we are going to sue someone. I asked him if this would change anything for him. He said that if it was a freak accident, then it did not matter but if your death was due to negligence, then we should press charges.

Michael wants me to promise him things. He wants to hold me accountable and to exert control over his little world. I told him that we are going through a journey with heaven as our ultimate destination. The one promise I can make is there is a heaven and that if he makes the right choices, he will go there and meet up with you again. Other than that, I can't promise anything.

157

As I continued to wait for answers about what caused Randy's heart attack, the thoughts of "why" and "how" were starting to occupy a bigger space in my mind. Trying to cope with the hurt, I'd revert to playing out Randy's worst-case health scenarios and my role when dealing with them. All I had to do was remember and relive the fear of a relapse, hiding the painkillers, the trauma of a respirator, or the anxiety of cancer. My musings gave me no relief. In fact, those trying times from our past seemed like child's play compared to the barrage of sadness and worries that now plagued the boys and me. All we wanted was for Randy to be with us again: whole, living and healthy Randy. While my husband lived, there was hope. With his death, there was nothing.

There was an emptiness, an unfillable void within me. I knew exactly how it felt to have a "heavy heart." Now I was that woman who could barely keep her head above the water. I was sinking into a bottomless crevasse. My chest was tightening. My heart was racing. If I knew that my sons would be fine without me, my deepest desire would be to leave this life to join Randy. The idea of fading away and disappearing into the mist felt far easier than grasping at the fragile gossamer tendrils of our frayed life, hoping against all odds I could weave them into something meaningful as we tried to live without Randy.

Except for Christian who was still clueless, what we all wanted was to be with him—in a place where we would not feel sharp endless pangs of sadness. Our entire family's joy and will to carry on was gone and my heart broke for all of us.

Again, I had to pray and trust that our needs would be met. To yield control over to Him actually felt liberating because I felt incapable of handling life and all its burdens on my own. Between the paperwork, business decisions and legal issues I was in such a state of anxiety that I'd beseech, "God, please help me out with all of this. Please give me the strength to deal with it all."

Jan 28 – Thursday

Dear Randy,

As I was putting Christian to bed, he was remembering you and things that he did with you. It makes me so sad to think he will not get to know you.

Adrienne and the girls took me out for some wine, cheese and to paint ceramics tonight. It was a lovely evening, a bandage that momentarily covers the huge void that sucks me down. Amy sees this more like a skin graft. A bandage will get old and fall off, but a graft will heal. This is a wound I will carry for the rest of my life, but I've got to believe it will heal and not hurt so much someday.

When my friends dropped me off back home, I remember thinking, "That was lovely, but I still do not feel happiness." My brain acknowledged the pleasure of their company and their thoughtful plan to distract me. Less than a month ago, that would have been a perfect outing: social, artsy and delicious. But I wondered if I would ever know what it was to feel happiness again.

Jan 31 – Sunday

Dear Randy,

It has been one month, but I've lived a lifetime of unimaginable sorrow, anxiety, grief and despair. And yet, I'm alive. After your mass last night, David had a meltdown. I probably caused it because I was overly harsh, but there was validity to his questions and feelings. I worry about him because he is mourning you with as much intensity as a young adult can— even though he is a little boy. He misses you terribly. Today was the first day I have not cried even though my heart aches badly.

David was only ten, but he had always been extremely mature for his age. Of the three boys, he was the closest to Randy. Even though I was clinging to my faith to get me through these times, he was voicing the same questions I asked myself:

- "Mom, why were my prayers for the last months and years not answered?"
- "What God would let me suffer this way? What God would take a father away from a kid?"
- "Why keep on living? What's the point?"

My eldest son was suffering. His life was turned inside out, and he could not make sense of a God who was incapable of healing his father, or who was indifferent to his prayers. We mirrored each other's grief and I saw myself in his deep black eyes. It was much harder to bear witness to his sadness because this was my child, my firstborn. I could empathize with David because I too was asking myself, "WHY?"

I thought we were "good" people. I could be fierce, but Randy did not have a mean bone in his body. We were giving and involved citizens and devout practicing Catholics. Far from perfect but surely better than drug dealers and criminals. Why would God allow all of this misfortune to befall us? In fact, was there even a God?

I began to wonder if He was a construct of our collective imagination, a way for humanity to "cope" with life being so difficult and uncertain. Until that point, I took my faith for granted and I never really questioned this inheritance. Randy's death shook the foundations of my beliefs. We had lived through past trials and they had prompted us to find balance, gratitude and faith. When we finally re-aligned as a couple and as parents, it was suddenly over. Was death the finality of Randy's soul? Was there truly a Heaven?

In the verdant tropical rainforest of my Panamanian childhood days, I remembered gingerly walking on a narrow suspension bridge to cross over a rushing stream and tumbling boulders. The notion of tripping and falling into the water was equally as exciting as it was terrifying. Our family's current journey was not too different from traversing that rickety wire, rope and wood plank bridge. We were swaying, unstable and, trying to get over to the other side. My example could make the hike a scary experience or one with the promise of discovery and accomplishment. How we would come out on the other side would depend on my attitude and beliefs. Faith could be a solid and integral part of our walk or it could be ephemeral like the misty clouds and fog of the rainforest highlands. I realized I had to fix my compass and center my axis, so I could guide the boys on this journey.

My beliefs were all over the map. At times I depended on God for strength and at other times, I did not know who He was at all. The love I had with Randy and my vision of how we would raise our sons together, our partnership producing beautiful work in photography and fashion, the notion of traveling and growing old with my husband had come to an abrupt end. As I leaned into God for strength and comfort, I also felt anger, confusion and much disappointment. How could I rely on God to take care of us when He had not delivered Randy from his ordeals? If my faith was shaken, what could I teach my sons? I knew I had to be careful about the conclusions I was drawing about my situation—who God was in my life and who He would be to them.

In the midst of my doubts, I remembered the desperate time when Randy's drug addiction and I met face to face. When that crisis became a burden that was too much for me to bear, I gave up and handed over the situation to Jesus. All of the problems I was trying to solve were beating me down. Once I surrendered to Him, I felt lifted through that time which had bogged me down. The power of that soul, body and mind experience was seared into my memory and kept me tethered to my faith.

"There are a lot of things that we are not able to understand about God" I answered truthfully to David's questions. "Death is one of those bad things that happen in this world, but we have to trust that there is a better place where there is no pain, and we have to hope that your father is there." Because of the strong religious foundation that the boys received at St. Paul, I did not have to explain the riches of heaven nor the ultimate sacrifice that our Lord had suffered for loving us. Death in a conceptual way had been defeated and David was clear on that. But who was God and what was Heaven were bigger questions that I could not answer for the boys or for myself.

I went to visit the Pastor at St. Paul's to talk about David and the many questions we both had: If God was Almighty, why did He not spare Randy? Or was it His mercy to spare our family from the suffering of a protracted demise or ongoing addiction problems? Either way, more than once I heard that "God has a plan" and it supremely irritated me because His plan was not to my liking. I needed some spiritual advice and it was comforting to talk to Pastor Jones.

Feb. 1 – Monday

Dear Randy,

We got the royalties check and it was great. You would have been so relieved and happy. However, it made me so, so sad. It's a relief to have the money to carry on, but the check was just a reminder that we can't do this together ever again. That was such a hard realization. You continue to take care of us. You live through your work and now, when I see your photos, I cherish the idea that I'm looking through your eyes. I shared this thought with David.

To never shoot photos with Randy again. To never share ideas, art direct or produce together was another loss that hit me when I opened the envelope and saw the check. Everything we did, from the kids' clothes to our vacations, were always with the photographs in mind. We even remodeled our house with the thoughts of sets and backgrounds. Life and work were completely interwoven and the fact that I was also losing this part of us was another blow to absorb.

Feb. 4 - Thursday

Dear Randy,

I keep reminding Christian about you. It pains me to think that he will forget you and that you enjoyed him so much. I hate to think that he will never know you. How unfair is that?!

I pulled up Pete's photo of you on the Brooklyn Bridge. His original one is full body—It hurt me so much to see all of you. I loved your entire person, your freckles, your hands, your eye wrinkles. I was reminded how you thought it was so cool to dress in cargo shorts and sneakers for work vs. executives in suits staying at the same hotels.

I still can't come to terms with the fact that you have died. You would have been so surprised at this outcome. I can't believe you are gone and that we will not have another moment together.

I had been a confidante to my friends many times, but my new vulnerability allowed them to open up even more in their efforts to console and show me their empathy. Now even mere acquaintances were willing to share memories or experiences they would normally not divulge . . . the loss of a parent at an early age, the death of a previous spouse, or their feelings about losing a child. In their sharing, I learned that keeping Randy's memory alive would be important for my sons. They would treasure hearing stories about him as their lives unfolded. As they reached new milestones like graduations, marriage, or the birth of their children, they would revisit their grief and mourn again. What lay ahead was daunting, but I was also given hope for the boys. The father of one of my friends had died when she was one month old, yet she spoke of him as if she had known him all her life. Her mother had kept his memory alive for her.

Just as I approached any of my previous life challenges, I reverted to my "de facto" mode . . . educating myself. Having been thrust into this unwanted journey, the best course of action I could think of was to learn about this most disheartening circumstance. My primary motivation was the children's wellbeing: how losing their father would affect them and how I could help them to cope and heal. I also needed to feed my faith, ground my beliefs and learn about that other destination—Randy's final adventure.

> *Feb. 6 - Saturday*
>
> *Dear Randy,*
>
> *I've been avidly reading the book that Nicola loaned me: Window to Eternity has given me great peace and serenity. I feel better knowing you are on a great journey and one of these days we will see you again.*
>
> *This morning I made David cry. Otherwise he would be taking out his frustrations on all of us—including Christian. It was better for him to cry.*

As I struggled to cope with our new reality, I realized I still had a gift for Randy. It would be my last but most important gift: How our children would know and remember him. I could choose the best memories, so the boys could look on him as he would have wanted. In the midst of my sadness I acknowledged this was one of the few luxuries I had by being the only living parent. I could have buried the saga of the addiction, but I made the very conscious decision not to repeat the errors of Randy's past. Our children would be fully aware of his struggles. Once Randy understood his addiction, the genetics, and his propensity to pass it on to our sons, he had been forthcoming to them about it all. I knew he would not have wanted me to "edit" this part of his history. They would also know need to know about his commitment, his love for them, and his goodness.

Feb. 9 - Thursday

Dear Randy,

"Dada takes me to mall."

"No touch water."

"Dada gives coin."

"Throw coin in water."

"No more coin."

Christian was clearly remembering our last visit to the Town Center where you were giving him pennies to throw into the fountain. It saddens me so much that he had so little time with you. I still have a hard time believing you are gone.

Going to the mall was much harder than I expected. There are so many memories attached to the places we went shopping for props and wardrobe. To think we will not go there together again, I will not hear your opinion—you won't ever compliment me again—is difficult. I am just too young to not have your love.

Our house was filled with souvenirs from our wanderings: Mexican crafts, Greek glassware, Australian boomerangs, South African carvings ... findings we carted from far flung places that gave character to our home alongside the many props we collected for our photo shoots. Randy was one of the few men I knew who actually looked forward to going to the local mall because shopping and scouting was an essential component of his work. In particular, he enjoyed the home décor stores, often finding items that enhanced the composition of his photos or added subliminal messages to the concepts we were visually conveying. He also monitored the clothes we would purchase because they had to be devoid of logos and be "on trend" with the color palate of the moment.

As I walked the corridors of the mall, my gut took another punch. One more thing I had taken for granted, a shopping companion who indulged me and found entertainment in an activity that lots of women enjoy, but most men barely tolerate. Like it or not, my new identity was being formed. I had no idea what would emerge, but I was painfully aware that yet another thing in my life would be forever gone.

I took a stab at tackling the bills, our taxes and the legal stuff. Meeting with my financial advisor, filing for Social Security benefits, scheduling an estate attorney, was a blur I barely remember. I was capable of gathering my senses and pulling myself together for an hour or two, but it took a supreme effort. After completing the task at hand, I was exhausted. Everything felt like heavy lifting and there was so much to do.

It never occurred to me that breaking down was an option or that I would be incapable of tackling life on my own. My three young sons needed me more than ever and I was all they had left. Being well-loved gave me the self-confidence I needed to carry on. That being said, the load felt overwhelming and I continued to sob over the adversities that lay ahead of us: the real ones I just had started to tackle and those that invaded my thoughts and paralyzed my brain when I pondered our future. Then when the anxiety became overwhelming, I turned to God for strength to wake up, get out of bed and get me through that day.

Tethered to Faith

"Faith is to believe what you do not see;
the reward of this faith is to see what you believe."

Saint Augustin

February 17

Dear Randy,

Today I found out that you died of coronary artery disease. I
spoke to the coroner who performed your autopsy. Your left
ventricle was enlarged, and you had arterial blockage. A piece
of plaque detached and occluded the artery that fed blood
to your heart. Everything else about you was fine—your liver,
kidneys, and your stomach. You were otherwise a healthy 45-
year old man.

I was stunned. As I asked my questions, I remember having to sit down in disbelief as he informed me that otherwise Randy was a healthy man for his age. No other major organ was damaged. No cirrhosis. No cancer. All his life Randy had complained about a sensitive stomach and even that was fine. A simple stent would have solved this issue. Of ALL the conditions tested at the hospital, this was the one the doctors never brought to my attention. I had spent hours researching lungs, kidneys, liver, and the digestive system. Each time they ran a test I educated myself about the procedure and what it could reveal, but the heart was the one rabbit hole I did not explore because no one pointed a finger.

To say that I had mixed emotions would be a gross understatement. My conflict was gargantuan. On one hand, Randy died in peace and I HAD to believe that he was in Heaven, fully restored. On the other hand, there were answers to his health conundrum with proven solutions that could have fixed his maladies. A stent could have given us the chance to get our lives back on track. If the 16 days at the hospital did not allow for his heart disease to be identified, was Randy's death the most merciful outcome? Or had we been robbed because a team of doctors missed something? Were they so focused on their specialty that they did not see the big picture? I needed to get back into the space of trusting God, of faith, and of Randy being in Heaven. This news re-opened wounds that were barely closed and the hurt started all over again . . . In my heart, I wanted to believe that God had spared Randy from more suffering in life, but I could not leave this stone unturned. I had to go through the motion of following up.

I immediately called Todd, my attorney friend who was helping me with all of the legal stuff. His wife Lisa was the PTA President that succeeded me and knowing he was in my corner was a huge relief. Once he heard my emotional recount of the conversation with the coroner, he suggested we meet with a few malpractice lawyers.

February 18

Dear Randy,

I had to deal with Blue Chip issues all over again, and I am also looking into selling the Porsche. I feel so sad to have to let go of the two things that you so loved; but I am clearly unable to keep them.

There is a possibility of a malpractice suit. If we win, the money will take care of much, but it also opens up the possibility that you could have been saved and none of this would have had to end this way. The boys would have a father and we would be together. I don't know if I should proceed. This could be very painful.

I keep going back to us and our love story. That is beautiful.

I was so used to Randy's long business trips that his being gone felt somewhat familiar but coming to terms with his death was surreal. To learn he was otherwise healthy was stunning. Many doctors, including a general practitioner and a psychiatrist, had seen him even prior to his hospitalization. There were ample opportunities for the physicians to have detected coronary artery disease, including the disclosure that his father had undergone a bypass not too long ago.

Because his heart was enlarged, it was not a recent issue but one that had been in the making for a long while. This explained his fatigue, loss of color, and the sensation of his heart bursting out of his chest which he expressed to me every so often in his last years. These symptoms mirror clinical anxiety combined with depression which was the psychiatrist's diagnosis. But he never felt sad and this explained why. I felt swindled. We both had been robbed of time, and the boys missed out on life as it could have been. We had worked so hard on our marriage and after getting to the place where we both needed to be, our flame was suddenly extinguished—our love story was over.

February 20

Dear Randy,

You are, were, the love of my life. I am feeling so sorry for myself. What if heaven is not true?

*The only thing that is sustaining me is the thought that you
are in a better place and are fully restored; that I will see you
again. But my faith falters and when that happens, I can't
contain the grief. Then everything is so wrong, and I feel so,
so cheated because I miss you so.*

I wondered if his death had spared us both the ever-present specter of addiction. Would that problem have continued to haunt us? I recalled the strange dream I had a few weeks before, where Randy's eyes had filled with tears of remorse as he showed me the white pills that were hidden. Was there meaning for me in that dream? Did it come to me in anticipation of these unexpected results? If our life was to be a prolonged battle against prescription painkillers, I knew I'd become unrecognizably estranged and hardened. And what would have happened to Randy? My soul was filled with peace in thinking about his spiritual growth in his last year. I felt he was at his highest point in that journey.

Until she shared with me, I was not aware that my friend Nicola had lost her first child, Hannah, when she was a 19-month-old toddler. While our circumstances were completely different, I could see in her eyes the depth of her loss and found someone who could relate to my pain. As our youngest children played together in the park, we talked, and she loaned me a book that could perhaps fill my spiritual drought. The author proposed that God did not intervene in some premature deaths for the good of the person's soul. In His infinite wisdom, with knowledge of our past, present and future, perhaps He allowed death because this outcome was the best for Randy, our children and me. I had no way of knowing what our future held but for sure, death from a heart attack seemed much more merciful and honorable than one from an overdose. I capitulated to the thought that it was better to grieve the loss of something beautiful and look forward to Heaven instead of growing into a bitter and disappointed woman.

Seeking answers to my questions about the reality of Heaven, about the notion of Randy being whole and healthy, and of us reuniting again, spurred me to pick up the one book that other countless souls had turned to for centuries. I started in Genesis—the beginning of the greatest story ever told. My reading had a purpose. I was on a mission to find out all that I could about God, Heaven and Jesus. Thankfully, because of my beloved nuns at Catholic School, I was well versed in the Gospels, and at St. Paul I had attended several Bible studies, so I was sufficiently equipped to undertake this exploration on my own. For me, faith and survival became intertwined and were a matter of existential importance on my path forward.

Venturing Out

"When I let go of what I am,
I become what I might be."

Lao Tzu - Chinese Philosopher

February 27

Dear Randy,

*I attended the Snowflake Gala last night. It was not as sad as I
expected, and I functioned OK.*

*I am able to talk and function on the outside, but the inside of
me is still in disbelief that this happened to us. How can it be
that our story has ended?*

he Snowflake Gala is one of the fundraisers I oversaw during my
PTA tenure. I remained on the Board as an Ex-Officio member
and still felt I had to support the school and my friends, many of whom
I had persuaded to join the board. I was a highly social creature and the
toll of the past months had limited my interaction with the community
that had been so supportive during these difficult times. It was weird

to attend a social event, but it felt right for me to touch base with my friends.

> *March 1*
>
> *Dear Randy,*
>
> *So, it is two months. It seems like such a short time, yet I feel I have lived a lifetime. I feel so, so ancient.*
>
> *I smelled your shirt today and it feels so real. I still can't believe you are gone. No matter how I try to rationalize your death, the sadness of what we had still remains.*

I would go through several hours in the day when all felt normal. And then suddenly, it would hit me that Randy was gone. What I would have given to see him again and share a moment. I was still bewildered about everything that had happened, but I dwelled less and less each day on the "why's"—reminding myself that God would take care of the boys and me.

> *March 9*
>
> *Dear Randy,*
>
> *I dreamt of you last night:*
>
> *Two rivers were flowing side by side. One was murky and the other was shallow and clear. I was in shallow water and suddenly, you were behind me—teasing me. I touched your chest and kissed you. You looked tanned and fit and very handsome. I remember being surprised.*
>
> *Seeing you in that dream made me feel very happy for you. You looked just like when we met. If I could have the boys remember you that way, it would be my triumph.*

Christian remembers the tricycle bell you showed him saying, "Dada put bell on Christian's bike."

Michael "revealed" to me how he makes himself dream. He said he programs his dream so it would be about you. He wishes to be in Catalina aboard Blue Chip. Finally, he is able to visualize you and say that he is sad.

All their dreams make me realize I have to meet each child right where they were: three different personalities and stages and levels of maturity. When Randy was alive, we could divide and conquer. He was willing to take the stance of disciplinarian while I could be the soft landing. Now, I had to morph both our roles into one: be caring, stand firm, as well as provide and chart the course. I had to be more empathetic and sensitive— qualities that were not my strong suit. This was going to require a level of emotional intelligence unknown to me at the time. I was inside an overwhelmingly dark tunnel with no light at the end in sight.

My father had returned to Panama, but my mom remained with us until mid-March. Life would never return to my version of "normal," but we started to adopt a routine and ease into our new existence. With the help of my manager and some friends, I showed the spring collection of my ETCETERA fashion line. I remember telling LeeAnne, "This is a hobby and I'm in no frame of mind for a hobby." I was ready to give it up, but she convinced me to do the show saying she would take care of the details. I just had to be present even though that felt to me like pushing a boulder up a hill. Of course, my girlfriends turned out in droves to support me and it was fun. Dressing the ladies, being social and keeping my mind busy was very therapeutic. Much to my surprise, my sales were amazingly high, so I ranked amongst the top three nationwide for my selling week. It was a big deal!

My numbers forced me to reframe my outlook. The wheels in my business head started to churn. I was counting on our royalties to see us through, but I was uncertain how long this would remain a possibility since photos, wardrobe, colors, etc. eventually age. My first choice was to continue producing commercial content, but I was not anywhere near Randy's skill level with the camera. Returning to my career in Corporate America would have twice orphaned my children, at a time when they most needed me to be fully present. That hamster wheel was very familiar to me and I knew it was not a viable option. Handed to me on a silver platter was a business that could also be a means to an end. ETCETERA could give me the opportunity to supplement our income or save for a rainy day while remaining flexible to the needs of my young sons. I remembered Randy's support and excitement for my first show in the fall, so I decided to turn this hobby into my new venture. Little did I know how much this choice would open doors and become an essential part of my life as we moved forward.

April 5

Dear Randy,

Michael's first birthday without you and our first Easter as well. Mom has been gone for one week and I am managing fairly well but I really miss you so much. Will I ever see you again?

With my mother's departure, I was the only adult in the house. The day did not have enough hours to accomplish all that had to be done. Given Randy's work travel schedule, I was well versed in the single mom rodeo, but it was a huge transition to step into my new life, our new normal. Having "survived" spring break on my own with three little boys felt like a huge accomplishment.

My favorite (and only) brother, Gene, came to visit us. We took Christian to Randy's favorite morning hangout. For a moment we thought the baby had forgotten about seeing his father because he was so well behaved while we were waiting for his donut.

> *April 20*
>
> *My love,*
>
> *A few days ago, Christian was actually able to verbalize an experience with you. He told me about your getting donuts for him but also "Dada buys a dark donut with candies." In other words, a chocolate donut with sprinkles. I was so happy that he remembered something that was six months ago.*
>
> *I decided to take him to Dunkin Donuts this morning and he was so, so, excited. As we approached the store, his eyes began to shine and he said, "Dada is in store!" I was not expecting this, and he was so happy. His little legs were kicking with excitement and he kept repeating "Dada is in store!"*

We sat down and after he took the first bite, Christian looked around and asked, "Where is Dada?" Gene and I looked at each other with difficulty. It broke my heart to tell him that his father would not be there . . . He was still too young to understand the concept of never, of death. Again, as we neared the Ft. Lauderdale airport to drop Gene off for his departing flight, Christian asked if we would be picking up Dada. The last time we both were there was when Randy took his trip to California, in October. He associated this airport with his father, a six-month-old memory.

> *April 30*
>
> *I paid a big chunk of the mortgage, titled the Porsche, and submitted your last photo shoot. I miss you so much. I'm exhausted by this new reality.*
>
> *I went to a parenting seminar the other day and it hit me hard*

to realize that I was a single parent. The sorrow is so deep that tears are not enough anymore. It has only been 16 weeks, but the days are so, so long.

Somehow, in the process of dealing with Randy's estate, I missed settling the title for his sports car. Todd, my attorney friend, realized my omission and had me rush to the DMV. I can't remember the details or his concerns, but this was a serious oversight. We just had to pray it would all proceed smoothly without raising eyebrows. As I was called up to the window, I handed the clerk Randy's death certificate. She took one look at me, said nothing, and proceeded to remedy my situation. As we wrapped up the transaction, she patted my hand and said: "It will all work out. I was in your situation 20 years ago." What were the chances that I'd land with a compassionate clerk who mirrored my circumstances? I felt as if my guardian angel was ahead of me, removing obstacles and paving the way.

Opening Randy's camera bag to retrieve his last photo shoot was something I had put off as long as I could, but his agency reminded me that I needed to send in his final submission. When we remodeled our home, we had converted one of the rooms into a studio and his office. I entered Randy's workspace with trepidation. There were so many memories inhabiting that corner of our house. The simple act of pulling the zipper of his camera bag was painful, rummaging through it to find the hard drives brought tears to my eyes. I darted in and out, efficiently grabbing what I needed. When I closed the door, I realized I was barely breathing and had to take a deep one.

Another impact happened when I attended a parenting seminar. As I listened to the lecturer speak about the importance of both parents aligning and communicating, it dawned on me I would no longer have to "get on the same page" with my spouse. His opinion and actions would be immaterial because I was the single parent left, it was all on me. The realization brought a lump to my throat and tears to my eyes.

Even though we had different perspectives and unifying our approach had been challenging, I would have gladly turned back the hands of time to have those conversations again.

Until seated, I had blissfully forgotten that Randy and I had both listened to the same speaker a year ago. Had I remembered that, I might have refrained from attending a very worthwhile lecture to avoid the memories that might assault me. Because I did not overthink most situations, I continued to be a participant in life. I mostly went through the motions of doing and living without too much analysis. Occasionally I'd be hit with an experience that was either no big deal (like the first time we went to the beach) or unforeseeably difficult. I learned to store the knot in a corner of my brain and unravel it when I was alone and could process my thoughts.

An acquaintance connected me with another woman who had lost her husband when her three children were young and similar in age to my sons. Kim visited me for a few hours that went by too fast. By the time her visit was over, I still had many questions that were unasked. The emotions, thoughts and challenges of losing a husband and a father bonded us in ways that can only be felt and understood by those who have shared a terrible tragedy. I was isolated in my grief because no one in my circle could empathize with a young widow. It was as if I had survived a plane crash and the closest anyone had ever experienced was a car accident. There simply was no comparison. But Kim knew exactly what I was feeling and understood my biggest concerns. She mentored me through this difficult period and gave me insight into the potholes and bumps that might be in my path.

"Deb, don't be surprised if some friends ask if you want to start dating again." I was shocked at the mere suggestion, but she explained that everyone wanted me to be happy and for some people, happiness meant finding another love. "Just be prepared and know that their intentions are good." Another insight was the confirmation that my time was going to be very limited. I'd be pulled in all directions, all at once, by life and my little people. "Be careful not to over exhaust yourself because you will ALWAYS be tired." I was already realizing there were not enough hours in my day to get everything done. "It is OK to let some things go, just manage each day at a time because your first year is going to be hard."

After I attended that seminar and talked to Kim, it dawned on me that I was an only parent. The realization was jarring, but it made my purpose crystal clear. It was up to me to advance our sons. I had a wonderful support system, but parenting was my load to carry until they were independent young adults. From here on, having this clarity of purpose allowed me to prune my life and shape it so as to fulfill this mission. It was as if my gardening shears were no longer for trimming, but for cutting off everything that was sticking out, so I could make myself smaller and more manageable. It showed what I had to give up and helped reveal what I could welcome or accept. I also realized that I had to be serene of mind and take extra care of my health because I could not go down.

My emotional state was so frail that I needed to find joy in life or at the very least, alleviate the pain and not upset myself. My nerves were not what they used to be, so any conflict or difficulty that I could have easily handled in the past just seemed magnified or unsurmountable. Our boat was afloat but could not be rocked—the keel was not deep enough to keep us stable. I began to pare down my relationships and avoid the ones that were stressful or negative. I could not go back to be the old Debbie. In the past I was more understanding and supportive, but I no longer had the bandwidth. Whatever reserves I had, were to be used for my children. David was much more sensitive, so I had to change the way I spoke to him, becoming much, much softer. Michael finally started to express his sadness and talk about Randy. Christian was still a toddler and it was up to me to keep whatever precious little memories were stored in his young heart.

A West Coast Sunset

"Blessed are those who mourn, for they shall be comforted."

Mathew 5:4

One of the strongest remnants of my Chinese legacy was my appreciation for food: its taste, its capacity to sustain life and its role in creating bonds over a shared meal. "You are what you eat" was one of the phrases I coined as I became a young mother and more acutely, when I embarked on Randy's health journey. He was a happy participant of the fast food, supersize me generation, whereas I disdained all it entailed. From the onset, I made our sons' baby food. David's first solid was a taro root mash, similar to the Hawaiian poi, followed by lentils. I mostly cooked from scratch, without shortcuts. It took love, energy and soul to feed my sons, to nourish their growing minds and bodies. I was running so low on every one of these elements that the gift of a meal was more than just food.

After spring break, I sent out an "update" email to my friends. It was helpful for them to know what was going on with me (inside and out) and writing continued to be therapeutic for me. I told them how exhausting it was to fly solo and how much I appreciated the care calendar that they set up for me. The help came in the form of meals— a true blessing in so many ways: time saved, stress of not having to run out at the last minute with 3 boys to the grocery store, the ability to plan and a cushion for the unexpected. If I did not shop while they were in school, I had to drag the three of them with me to the supermarket . . . a scenario no mother enjoys. I was wound up so tightly that snapping was just one emotion away, so the meals afforded a little bit more flexibility and gave me time to adapt to my new normal.

May 10

Dear Friends and Family,

Widowhood. It is such a tragic statement to my new identity which is what I have been trying to figure out these days. All I can think of is the parable of the gnarled old widow whose offertory coins were more precious than anyone else's because she had so little to give.

I never thought I would be that person. In fact, I catch myself thinking "that poor woman" and then, I realize that person is me. I finished reading this wonderful book called "A Grace Disguised" by Jerry Sittser which I recommend to anyone who has suffered a loss . . . any loss: divorce, work, home, etc.

Another big step was starting to clean out Randy's studio. His space had become a catch all, like an indoor, messy garage. I can't say I've made much progress, but I'm pleased with what I have done. Some corners are harder than others. There are so many memories attached to his space, but at least I have the illusion that I will take up photography and so I can justify keeping it all as it has always been. It will take me many months to turn it into what I want, but that is OK. There is no rush.

Mother's Day was better than I had expected. My cousins, Michelle and Jaden, visited for the weekend and we celebrated with Aunt Pat and her family. I received a call from Duwayne, our best man and a gift from Frances. We chose so well, for all of our six godparents have been there for me in so many ways.

I miss my husband. As much as I wonder why him, why us, why me, I am thankful for all of the support I have from family and friends. I am saddened when I think of how much Randy loved life and looked forward to living it fully again. His last month was so difficult and I wish he did not have to suffer so much. I keep going back to September when all was so good for him on many levels. To think that his death is final is unbearable, but I am filled with hope when I believe that death is only a pathway to our ultimate and true destination. If this is the case, then Randy was truly ready to go and that gives me so much peace. I pray to remain in this frame of mind because then all is just a matter of time and work for me.

I know I will never be the same person again and I am beginning to be comfortable with that reality. In fact, I would hope that I could remain consistently detached from the things of this world and focus on the things that matter for eternity. It is my hope that as I share this journey with you, that you are also changed by my circumstances and allow any sorrow and sadness that you feel for me to affect your life in a positive and permanent way.

The need to be calm was imperative. My mood directly influenced the boys' behavior and they were so much better off if I was serene. They were having unexplained headaches and stomachaches which I have read is symptomatic of grief. I started to learn how to be numb while also being empathetic to their feelings. It was not easy for me to balance the acknowledgement of their pain and also remain calm and detached, but our circumstances were compelling me to develop this ability. It would take years to master this skill, but through no choice of my own, I was already on the path and walking on hot stones.

Christian was back to napping somewhat regularly which was a HUGE relief. He also started to attend a twice-a-week Pee Wee Power Hour which gave me a bit more time to take care of everything I had on my plate. In the three hours to myself I was capable of running to the post office, two libraries, a bookstore, the bank, and getting a haircut. Now, THAT was true time management. In addition, friends transported the older boys to school (a big help), and my wonderful neighbors were always ready to lend a hand, especially with Christian. It was definitely taking a village to get us through this difficult time.

I presented my fourth fashion collection and thus completed a whole year with the clothing line. This time my mom was not around so I counted on the priceless support of friends and neighbors who helped with the boys. I truly enjoyed the focus that the business required and its social aspect. For brief moments, I wished I could do this all day because it was such a distracting and consuming effort, and it was so removed from my everyday routine and new reality.

As soon as school was out, my cousin Jaden took the older boys to Jensen Beach, so I could drop Christian off with my parents in Panama. I also had to clean up our house in California to get it ready for sale and it would be an easier task without a toddler along. The logistics of leaving the older boys in Florida while I flew to Panama would have been complicated without Jaden's help. She did not have children of her own and was somewhat apprehensive about taking on the soccer mom role. I had a moment of panic when the airline cancelled my return flight and I lost an entire day waiting for the next one, but David and Michael were well behaved, and they all had a pleasant time. This was one of the many examples of learning to juggle—while riding a unicycle balanced on a high-wire in the circus of my life.

Going from having it all, from being the person who was everyone's helper, to asking for support could have been demoralizing and uncomfortable. I was deeply conscious of the many "favors" I received and could never reciprocate. I was not used to feeling this way. My role from being the doer and lead volunteer had suddenly reversed. Now I was heavily reliant on the kindness and goodwill of my community. In a moment of spiritual insight, I realized this role reversal was a mutual blessing: it revealed the fruits of my past generosity while becoming a means to allow moments of grace to those who were supportive.

June 16

Dear Friends and Family,

We have now been in California for a little over two weeks. It has been undeniably difficult for the boys me and. I knew that facing summer and June would represent a new phase in our mourning. This month contains the celebration of our wedding anniversary (15 years) and Randy's 46th birthday. In the past, I managed the school year months, our Boca life and our familiar routine. Summer was always full of travel and making plans with Randy. California, in particular, is very hard because the West Coast is all about him and this is our first time here without his guidance.

During the first few days, I could clearly feel the power of prayer. I know for sure that at least four of you were praying for me as I faced what is left of our California life. This must have been what saved me from sinking into the awful sorrow and despair that comes with facing such an intense reality. It is so enveloping that all you can do is beg for mercy, to be numbed, and to be delivered from the sadness. I would not wish this feeling on anyone. It did not last long, but while I was in its midst, it was almost as bad as right after Randy died.

The boys and I did the things we used to love doing with Randy. We bought real beef jerky from Mahogany Smoked Meats in Bishop, our favorite store. The boys spent a good amount of their savings on the dried meat ($34 per pound) which they love. At those prices I told them that the beef jerky needed to last a whole year! We visited the Ancient Bristlecone Forest which is home to the oldest living things on Earth. There are trees there that are four or five thousand years old, surviving at over 9,000 feet altitude. We also went to the very aptly named Death Valley where the boys learned to have a new appreciation for water.

This trip was a new experience for me. It was challenging to be able to do it alone, scary to be the only driver, and a burden to be the only adult. It was sad but beautiful to relive past travels and share them with the boys. I won't be doing this again anytime soon. Maybe when Christian comes of age so he can also experience these places, although Death Valley may not happen—twice in a lifetime is enough. I went to Palm Springs with the boys and my in-laws. They had fun hiking and collecting fool's gold. Now I am back in Huntington Beach finishing the packing and getting ready for a garage sale on Saturday.

Please keep us all in your prayers as the 18th is Randy's birthday. The boys and I will be celebrating with a mass and dinner at the Spaghetti Factory, an old favorite of ours. We will be back in Boca shortly after.

I dreaded heading out to California, but it was necessary. I knew it was going to be emotionally difficult, and I did not foresee us returning for a long while, so this was a "do it all" trip. I had to cement the boys' memories, see their grandparents, and deal with our West Coast assets. While I was merely executing decisions Randy and I had already made about our beach house and boat, it never entered my mind that I would also be finding and packing up his cross-country travel maps, camping gear, surfboard and clothes. Cleaning out all of his belongings was daunting, and reality hit me like a punch in my face. I was saying goodbye to Randy's happy place, to his youth, and to all that he embodied: the free-spirited adventurer that had captured my heart. In Florida, I had the ability to do things at my own pace, when I felt I could handle it, but in California I was in a time crunch because the house would be up for sale in July.

As I sifted and sorted through his stuff, deciding what to toss or ship to Florida, I found his handwritten notes and photography filters. Touching these inanimate objects brought me to tears. I used to call Randy "Filter Faris" because he used them to create beauty in a skyline that would have been otherwise ordinary. It was the main tool in his bag of tricks for capturing landscapes. His camping equipment was neat and in order, minimal because he wanted to be comfortable but efficient. He had a 20-year-old lantern that was still in perfect working condition. So many tendrils of all we did together.

Even before his hospitalization crisis, Randy had already decided to sell Blue Chip, his beloved Grand Banks boat and in some way or the other, we would give up the beach house. We had acknowledged the boys were old enough to see more of the world and we had extensively "done" California. The great ocean crossing from Newport to Santa Barbara and the Channel Islands was checked off his bucket list and he no longer harbored life goals on this side of the country.

California was the repository of "doing" memories. Randy was vibrant when he was on the West Coast, and in his last years, it was all about giving the boys the legacy of his youth while acknowledging that our real life was in Florida. It was so sad to say goodbye in such a palpable and tangible way. This was different. It was farewell to an era and a landscape that had shaped Randy into the man he had become. In moments of sadness, I had to remind myself of our past conversations. I was simply executing the details of the decisions we had already made.

David had a rough moment about four days into our visit. Michael was annoying him which triggered his reaction. Normally he could handle his sibling's provoking him, but the memories out there were just too intense. He was furious at God, questioning again, "What kind of God would create sin and death by planting a tree of knowledge.?" I told him that "Death is due to sin, not God's plan" but he took it further, making God responsible for creating sin. He was so, so, so angry. My consolation was that being so angry must mean he has a relationship with God. I told him, "I am also angry, and it is OK to express it, but my anger is why God did not allow Daddy to live or to be healthy." There are some things that we will never fully understand.

A big relief was taking the boys down memory lane to Lone Pine, at the base of Mt. Whitney. This was my first camping experience in the civilized world, as opposed to hacking down grass and shrubs in Mexico or Venezuela with a machete. The three of us put the tent up together and did not buy groceries or go to a restaurant for four days. We were only going to camp two nights, but we extended our stay by popular demand. After a hike on our last morning, we returned to a wind-swept tent which had been rescued by some thoughtful fellow campers. It was time to leave and find breakfast because we were totally out of food supplies, but they invited us over to their site joining them for a gourmet meal of eggs benedict. This unexpected treat was one of the many instances of "the Lord provides" that we would encounter in our journey.

It felt like such an accomplishment to do this adventure solo, without Randy at my side. Camping was his thing, not mine, but the cool dry weather, lack of bugs and beautiful vistas made it bearable and actually enjoyable. On our first night, Michael cried softly which was new to me because I had never seen Michael shed a tear. Since then I learned that he did it at night, always very privately, just like me.

I had been somewhat apprehensive about a camping adventure as a single woman with two small boys, but felt certain that either Jesus, Randy or my guardian angels would look out for us. And my cleaning lady was in agreement. She was supposed to check on our house a week later following our departure, but "something" made her swing by the day after we left. Much to her dismay, she found my house and car keys on the ledge leading towards our front door . . . an open invitation to rob our home. Her first remark to me was, "That husband of yours gave me a nudge to get over to the house." She had always been very fond of Randy.

Another small wonder were the flowers. One of my friends had brought over an orchid when Randy was sick. Her life and mine had intersected in interesting ways. We both served on the PTA and had been Presidents. We both had chaired the auction event, and notably, she was the prior owner of my clothing franchise. We had a further connection, Debbie (we even shared our name) was David's 5th grade teacher. Normally the lifespan of an orchid bloom is six to ten-weeks, but her flowers lasted well into six months, much beyond their normal expiration date. I noted their longevity around Easter and was delighted to still have them around. Before we departed to California, three of the blooms were still vibrantly alive and I realized that our wedding anniversary, Father's Day and Randy's birthday were still pending. The final one dropped soon after we returned, right after Randy's birthday. It was a small event that held great awe for me.

July 18, 2010

Dear Randy,

How can life have taken you away so soon? I wish we had more time together. Just you and me, like the very old couples, content with each other's company. Like when we were in Sidney, at the Lord Nelson, or when you showed me the Milky Way out in the Australian Outback. So much left to see and do, just you and me.

I wish we had been able to say goodbye. I know you are on the other side, waiting and that I must do what I must here. I have a lot of work but my heart longs to be with you. I am so glad you were spared a nursing home. You would have hated assisted living. I'm happy for you.

Within a few days of returning to Florida, we packed our bags again and headed to reunite with Christian in Panama. We would spend some time at my parent's country home. In a curious twist of circumstances, after many years away and abroad, they had returned to the verdant tropical highlands of my childhood to retire and built a beautiful home nestled amongst the lush rainforest coffee plantations. The smell of earth, the tingling of cool air, and the rich vegetation were a soothing balm to my frayed psyche. My parents doted on the boys and entertained them, allowing me some much-needed solitude and the time to continue reading the Bible.

I remember walking down the dirt road in front of their home and clearly "hearing" God's voice. It is difficult to describe this experience: soundless words delivering short concise responses with the clarity of a perfectly tuned radio station. I had the awareness to know this channel had opened up because of my intense grief. Somehow, I was also cognizant it would not be the same when my life returned to some semblance of normal. Static would invade this connection and opaque its clarity, so I knew I had to cherish the experience with awe and gratitude.

The Yellow House

"In my Father's house there are many dwelling places;
if it were not so, I would have told you;
for I go to prepare a place for you."

John 14:2

ummer was almost to an end. We returned much rested to Florida and ready to embark on a new school year. I still cried almost every night, when I was alone, and the house was quiet. I was overwhelmed with the future because the dark tunnel with no glimmering end in sight was becoming uneasily familiar. In the past, I could plan vacations and the logistics of it all, but now I could barely look farther than one week ahead. When your life has been yanked like a rug pulled from under your feet, it takes a while to get over the shock and bruises. All of my life visions and plans had evaporated, so I did not have the courage or imagination to plan for anything beyond a couple of days.

August 8, 2010

Dear Randy,

I was cleaning up the studio and I found a bottle of Hydrocodone dated 12/23 hidden inside a prop. I can only imagine the pain you must have felt, and it makes me so sad that you were so tortured.

I know that MY Randy would have never wanted this sorrow and THAT life for me or the boys. God must have been merciful with you and me for He delivered us from that life . . . you are no longer mired in the sadness and hopelessness of your addiction.

Finding this painkiller was not as earth shattering as it would have been in the past, during the stage when we were dealing with his addiction. If I had found it then, it would have led to a huge fight and much drama. But now, all I felt was pain and compassion. When discussing the lung biopsy with his surgeon, we raised the issue of a relapse from the painkillers they were planning to prescribe. The surgeon was unequivocal, "You WILL need painkillers after this surgery" which left us with a no-win situation: find out if he had lung cancer and brave the relapse or do nothing at all. There really was no choice for us.

After his surgery, Randy had hidden this medication and I would have never known why . . . except the answer was within the vivid dream I had months ago. I finally understood his entire message which I had journaled, but I could not comprehend: Randy was sorry that our life together had been truncated, but life with the specter of addiction looming over us would have been an infinitely worse alternative. He must have known that I would eventually discover these hidden pills and found a way to come through so that I could be prepared. With his tears, Randy had asked for my forgiveness and understanding before I even had the chance to get angry. He was taking care of me from beyond and it must have taken a lot of strength for him to come through in that way.

I was beyond tortured that such a good soul like his had experienced intense physical and emotional anguish. My memories were so full of glimpses of the real Randy, the one who loved me so, so much. Those pills in my hand were a reminder of the "Shadow," when he was diminished, listless and drawn. I wished life had been different for us and our good times together were longer, but I was increasingly certain Heaven was real and that he left us when his soul was indeed ready.

After his third and last rehab visit, he was exceedingly understanding of the pervasive nature of the painkillers, the role of genetics and the triggers that caused a relapse. He respected the process and when healthy, his inclination and addiction seemed as if they were a thing of the past. The key to this whole conundrum was "when he was healthy" because in that state, Randy had the strength to fight and the presence of mind to be wary. In this convoluted health journey, the misdiagnosis of his coronary artery disease vs. anxiety and depression had left Randy exposed and vulnerable.

It was a mystery inserted into an enigma because we were dealing with two issues: addiction and heart disease. If he was unable to overcome the addiction, living in the hopeless specter of that shadow would have been hell for him and purgatory for me. As unfair as it felt, under these conditions, his death was truly the most merciful outcome.

Both David and I still had vivid dreams about Randy. I saw images that later on would come to fruition. They were reminders that all was OK, and we were not alone. I shared some of my dreams with the boys because I wanted them to understand that Heaven was not some ethereal place, up in the clouds. It was real and relatable—just different in ways that we could not understand. When they asked about their father, I'd say, "Daddy is just preparing our house in Heaven. It probably has a lot of woodwork because he loves carpentry."

David mourned his father with the heart of a child and the mind of an adult. He had asked the deeply insightful and tough questions . . . the same ones I had asked myself. It was only appropriate that he received a vivid dream which revealed to him that his father was healthy and restored. I prayed these experiences reinforced his faith if it ever faltered as he grew older. David mentioned he had seen a yellow house in his dreams, but I did not make the connection with the one I had "seen" except they were both the same color. One day, as we were driving on the main street in Boca, we looked at each other with surprise. Right in front of us was an oversized yellow British Colonial cottage that caught our attention. We had never taken much note because it was hidden behind the foliage, but in a strange coincidence, this house looked just like the one that was both in his and my dream.

Christian had this photographic memory, just like his father. I found myself taking him to the library farthest from our home, the one that we rarely visited. As we entered, he remarked: "Do you remember when Daddy brought me to the "libely!" (He still had not mastered the pronouns and enunciation). "I thought we were buying books. I walked next to Daddy and sat in the brown chair." This memory was over one year old, but accurate. I prayed he would hold on to it.

August 29, 2010

Dear Randy,

My birthday was as good as could be. A few weeks ago, I asked our neighbor to take the boys shopping so they could get me a "surprise" gift. David was so sweet when he gave it to me at dinner, kneeling down before me. He is such a good-hearted boy. I hope life and his future girlfriends are kind and don't break his heart.

Michael could not contain himself and gave me his present the day before, but he tried to mislead me by asking what I wanted for my birthday—trying to make me believe that he had nothing. He is such a trickster.

My godparents took me out for lunch and some neighbors treated all of us to a beautiful dinner at a restaurant overlooking the Intercoastal. It was not an easy day, but then again, it was not as hard as it could have been. As August was about to end, I started to gear up to remember September, which was Randy's last wonderful and perfect month. It was a time when I had experienced his full potential as a husband, father and person. He was ready to get back to work, help out with my new business and he was great with the boys. Randy was content with life and his greatest ambition was to see his sons grow up. He was no longer chasing achievement. Life was once again a gift. After September, our candle got snuffed out—too soon and in a horribly wrong way. Somehow, I had to free myself of the anger and sense of injustice in order to accept that it was the best outcome.

As we entered the routine of the new school year, I remember walking out of the YMCA and feeling incredibly at peace and grateful. I was certain someone was praying for me because I could feel the invisible "balm" coating my existence, like a shield that allowed me to see through but not feel too intensely. I was grateful my life was manageable on a daily basis and I could afford to continue being a stay at home mother. As I contemplated my children, part of me wanted them to grow up quickly so that I did not have to bear the responsibility of raising them solo, but the other part of me just wanted them to remain little boys. The older ones seemed to not miss Randy as much, which was hard, but best for them as their children's instinct for survival took over. Christian still did not understand the concept of death and imagined his father on a long and far-away trip.

Unless it was absolutely necessary, like selling the California beach house, I was told to postpone any major decisions for at least one year. After such a momentous loss, I would need time to process and let the trauma subside so that my choices were not made under duress. As I acknowledged the level of help I was receiving from my community, the support from my neighbors, and the protective cocoon that our memory-laden home afforded us, I was more and more compelled to remain in Boca Raton. My parents had generously offered that we could move to Panama, but the boys' future was here in the US. I had to find a way to make it all work and I was starting to feel increasingly confident it was possible.

My parents had instilled their values by example. They were judicious with their lifestyle and spending habits. For instance, despite my father's success, we remained in the same home they bought upon arriving to Venezuela. Instead of indulging in luxuries, my they chose to enrich our lives with knowledge and cultural experiences. This philosophy of personal growth rather than material accumulation allowed them to effectively move their assets out of the country mere days prior to the fateful Black Friday which plunged the country into a recession that never reversed course. Having witnessed that economic downturn, I was mindful about being financially prudent and was comfortable pairing our life down to meet our new circumstances. I was strict about not dipping into our savings, but some months were tough, tempting me to deviate from my policy.

In different ways, each day I was comforted and encouraged by small blessings that reminded me God was taking care of us. Sometimes it was the perfect book suggested by a mere stranger, an out-of-the-blue phone call, or the surprise check that completed the monthly budget shortfall. At one point, I had an unforeseen expense that landed me $613 in the red. Much to my surprise, I received an unexpected check from a job that I had done a long while ago. I had translated a two-minute conversation and did not expect any compensation for this favor, never imagining I would receive a $610 check years later. Skeptics would call this a coincidence, but clearly it was not such. Little incidents such as this one sprinkled my life with astonishment and wonder. They happened on a regular basis and because of them, I knew I was not alone.

It was around this time that I was well into reading the Bible from the beginning and had passed the 2/3 mark. Upon arriving to Acts (of the Apostles) I was reminded about the terrible persecution, horrific torture and grizzly deaths the early followers of Christ endured because of their faith and beliefs. I realized those people were witnesses to events that altered their existence; events that thousands celebrated every year. Somehow the passage of time and the rites of religion had varnished over the guts and grit of their reality. Those early Christians saw "something" that transformed their belief, so they were willing to die for what was beyond this life. Between my personal experiences and the historical records of their suffering, I knew that if 500 plus people were willing to endure a terrible death, then my faith in Jesus and His resurrection was built on a solid foundation. This realization allowed me to stop questioning and receive with full openness the many graces that touched our lives. What most would deem as chance, luck, or surprising coincidences, I could fully acknowledge as God given favors.

September 17, 2010

Dear Randy,

I mourn what is not and what could have been if you were healthy. I'm filled with infinite sadness thinking of what we did not do together. God helps and comforts me.

I had to dig deep to find courage to meet the attorney who was looking into Randy's case. She was very well respected in the legal community. After an initial review, there was sufficient merit to proceed forward. On one hand, this was encouraging because Randy's medical ordeal never felt quite right, so this meeting confirmed all the uneasiness and doubts I felt about his care. Her assessment vindicated my intuition. On the other hand, I had already accepted this death was his best possible outcome. Because of what the dream had revealed, Randy exited with dignity and I could be at peace. Having this perspective proved to be the healthiest approach because months later I was told that Randy's case was probably unwinnable, so her office was no longer going to pursue it. Had our situation occurred ten years prior, I would have been awarded a few million dollars, but in the current legal environment, on top of incompetence, they had to prove the intention to commit malpractice.

November 30, 2010

Dear Randy,

Well, Thanksgiving went rather well but I was preparing for it. We went to Disney's Hollywood Studios on Wednesday which marked one year since you were admitted into the hospital. We overnighted at Jaden's and spent the next day with her. I was OK until it was time to drive home and the sadness started all over again.

I feel I have lost the zest for life and I so wish it was all over. I have so many questions when I see God. Why did you have to endure so much? I see how He blesses us on a daily basis, but why did this have to happen to us? When I arrive, will you be there to greet me and say, "Hi Beautiful?" I miss you so much.

As the calendar pages turned to December, one year after the hospitalization trauma, I had a few more dreams about Randy. They gave me happiness and made me feel good when I woke up, but I recognized they were just dreams—and not visits. In one, I only saw the back of Randy's head, but I knew he was present. In another, we were high schoolers, a time when we did not know each other in real life. They all were noted in my journal. However, there was one exception that felt singularly different, even though it happened while I was sleeping:

I was talking to a friend about dinghies and suddenly you appeared, hoping that David remembered all that you had taught him about an outboard. We then shifted locations and were both in innertubes, floating through thermal waters.

- I asked you, "Are you happy?"

- You said, "I miss you."

- I replied in a comforting way, "You'll see me someday."

- And you completed with, "When you are done with the boys."

Our marriage had been deeply flawed, but we loved each other in ways that transcended time and space. Ours was a love that allowed us to be very independent individuals. We did not "compete" with each other. Instead, we "complemented" one another. Randy was with me in the ordinary moments of life. Our souls were united regardless of time, and we would see each other again.

December 21, 2010

Dear Randy,

Christian has discovered the power of a phone call. After saying hello to Adrine, he managed to get us invited over for dinner by just asking her. I told him to take care of the maraca that you brought him from Spain and soon after he told me:

- We need to call Daddy by phone.

- What are you going to tell him?

- I'm going to tell him to buy me another maraca.

Sadly, I had to tell him that we could not reach you by phone.
He talks about going to the airport to pick you up or about
your being in the Yellow House in Paradise.

As Christmas approached, at any given moment I was consumed with dread. But thankfully my condition of numbness usually returned quickly. I knew the month of December was bound to be laden with emotion so I asked Debbie Stine, one of my powerful prayer warriors, to plead on my behalf. She was definitely heard because soon after I made my request, my anger at being left "holding the bag", dialed down and subsided.

I continued to read the Bible avidly, looking for clues into the afterlife and descriptions of Heaven and the other realms. I desperately needed to know and feel where Randy's soul might be as I yearned to be there myself. If I ever had any fear of dying, it was gone. Life had become a training ground for my ultimate destination. I just needed a reminder of where I wanted to end up, coupled with the strength and help to fulfill my purpose with the boys.

When I looked at the beautiful Christmas cards we were receiving, I felt pangs of regret that our family would never again participate as subjects in Randy's creative photo shoots. In the last few years, one of our Christmas traditions was to photograph the boys as if we were producing a commercial advertisement. I decided to send cards after we experienced the season for our first time without him. Considering it all, the children were doing well, but I was somewhat frustrated to be the only parent around.

My status was evidently clear as we put together our artificial Christmas tree. I had never done it before because my department was decorating—not assembling. I loved that tree. Randy went to three Lowe's in the area to find that particular one . . . just because I wanted it. I missed my husband who indulged all of my eccentricities and whims. David and Michael were very much into the holidays and decorated the house themselves. The tree turned out lovely and gaudy at the same time, but it was theirs and to them it was perfect— I agreed. They were very excited about Christmas. Thank goodness this season was not marred in their memory. Michael fluctuated from extreme emotions to calmness. David had become less angry and his emotions were more stable. I felt heartbroken for Christian who did not know how to be sad and would never know how much he had missed.

In the midst of what had been the most painful year of my life, my relationship with God was transformed. He did not take away my problems or deliver easy solutions but was unequivocally at my side, giving me a nudge, or even carrying me. This story was a fitting analogy to my situation:

A man sits at the top of his house's roof, hanging on for dear life and imploring that God may save him from the rising waters. A neighbor rows by and yells "Jump in and you can share the canoe with me." He declines by saying, "No worries. God will save me." Moments later, a helicopter flies atop and they throw out a lifeline which he refuses—waiting for God to save him. Finally, the waters sweep him away and the man drowns. As he wakes up in Heaven, he asks, "God, why did You not save me?" God replied, "My son, I sent you a canoe, then a helicopter…"

I was still unsure how I would tackle life and I missed being loved by Randy, but I had the certainty that God was easing my worries, throwing me lifelines, and sustaining our family as I navigated through troubled waters. Small and unexpected wonders showed up as flowers, objects, words and even money let me know that I was not alone. I just had to be sufficiently aware to recognize God's guiding hand, hear the whispers of the Holy Spirit, and feel the love that Jesus had for me when I was empty.

A New Normal

"More than that, we rejoice in our sufferings,
knowing that suffering produces endurance, and endurance
produces character, and character produces hope"

Romans 5:3-4.

Christmas was actually great. My parents flew in and we had a quiet, peaceful and enjoyable dinner with Amy's family. This was Christian's first "real" Christmas because he finally understood the holiday and the concept of presents. Michael remarked this one was his best ever, probably because he got an i-Touch and the Elder Wand. He coveted but did not expect to receive these gifts. David was content with his gourmet food, including a box of Kobe beef steaks. A Secret Santa lavished our family with presents during the four days prior to Christmas. We woke up every morning to a few gifts left on our doorstep, making the season even more magical for my little people.

January 9, 2011

Dear Friends and Family,

If you ever wonder what it feels like to be prayed over, I'd say that it is like a 2 inch thick coat of Karo Syrup that shields your soul and numbs you from life. You can see through this bubble, but you are protected and cushioned while you are in it. It is like being in a focused, deliberate state of denial where nothing gets to you. Thus, I am grateful for what all of you collectively accomplished during the last few weeks for the boys and me.

Your thoughts and prayers surrounded me through the tangible evidence of e-mails, cards, kind words and hugs.

Some of you don't know what to say, but we have been in your hearts during the last few weeks. I myself would not know what to tell another grieving woman so believe me, I totally understand your loss for words. I just want you to know this: Prayers are felt. What should have been the re-living of a terrible time was made bearable for me and OK for David and Michael.

I am touched by the fact that friends from distant times and places still remember us and find the time to reach out. I'd like you to know that when you do so, you are present in my thoughts as well as my memories. I think warmly about the experiences that bonded us. I hope that this message conveys how thankful I am that we have met.

On December 31st, Randy's one-year anniversary, I was very edgy—not knowing what to expect. How would we honor and remember Randy on this day? Each one of us wrote down our thoughts and attached our messages to some bottle rockets. It was David's idea to use firecrackers to send them up to Heaven. Randy would have been amused because he loved to build a fire. We lit and sent them off after a quiet dinner with some good friends, my parents and my newlywed brother and sister-in-law. I wanted the day to be enjoyable for the boys without being festive and I managed this well enough.

I was astonished that one year had already passed. My first year felt quick and eternal at the same time. After a gut twisting experience, it seemed that many lifetimes had coursed through the fibers of my body. I had been a health advocate, nurse, and caretaker. . . not to mention an accountability partner, counselor, pharmacist and nutritionist when dealing with Randy's addiction issues.

Just barely into my early forties, I had played roles that most wives, including my own mother, aunts, and older friends had yet to consider. I had already crossed the threshold of widowhood when most women had not even thought of going down that hall and opening that door. . . a knob that no one wants to touch. Feeling ancient beyond my years, I had learned to carry my sorrow, accept the hole in my heart and while I dreaded the thought of a second, third or fourth year, I also learned to not overthink the future and to live in the present— just one day at a time.

Unlike those widowed later in life, I had little time for introspection because I was busy with the boys, maintaining our home and mindfully taking care of myself. As an only parent, staying healthy and fit transcended my wellbeing. It was a matter of survival because if I went down, so would our whole unit. Working out was the only "me-time" that I did not give up. Exercising strengthened my muscles and bones (I'm a poster child candidate for osteoporosis), flooded my body with endorphins and built up the stamina I needed to stay in the race.

February 11, 2011

Dear Randy,

Liz is here to visit, and it has been wonderful, I feel like I'm getting so much done. Her company is soothing and has given me a break, but I also have time to be sad and think of you again.

I'm nearing the end of the Bible and have been reading a lot about the Apocalypse, the end of times. Who knows when that will happen, but the notion is not frightening to me. I do look forward to the yellow house in Heaven.

Liz was an old friend who came to help me when David was first born, bridging the gap while I figured out child care during my career years. She had visited us many times and the children loved her. Her presence allowed me time to get off the hamster wheel and catch my breath. I was also able to finish my quest to read the Bible from beginning to end.

My new normal had begun to unfold and with it came a detachment from life as I had known it. I felt like a visitor with a purpose, but my true home was somewhere else. Increasingly, I contemplated life as a temporary assignment. A good analogy would be my fondness for Hawaii. Between our honeymoon and many other visits, I was incredibly drawn to these Pacific islands. Their tropical and lush vegetation reminded me of Venezuela and Panama, including the deep contrast between the high mountains and ocean, but the weather was pleasantly drier and cooler. Whereas I was a minority everywhere else, in Hawaii the confluence of Asian, European, and native influences was commonplace . . . I was one of many and did not stand out. These islands perfectly suited our sensibilities. Better yet, I was able to surf the long waves of Waikiki with Randy. For a time, when he was working there, we even entertained the notion of buying some property because Hawaii was idyllic to both of us. I never tired of visiting this paradise on Earth, but it was always with the full knowledge that our home was somewhere else. My new normal was a magnification of this feeling. I sought to find joy while I fulfilled my purpose here on Earth but deep inside, my soul knew that Heaven was my ultimate destination. I knew the last breath I would take in this life would mean that I had returned to my real home, and this hope gave me immeasurable peace.

On March 11, the world was taken aback as a powerful earthquake in Japan unleashed a wide swath of destruction, tsunami waves and a nuclear disaster. As images of the devastation started to reach us in the days and weeks that followed, I could only imagine the loss that countless ravaged Japanese families were facing. In the blink of an eye, thousands were orphaned and widowed. Many of the elderly lived with their families and had lost their children and grandchildren. There was no one left to care for them. I was deeply affected by what I was seeing from afar because I knew only too well how it felt to have my life swept away. However, as unfair as my situation seemed to me, it was nothing compared to the destruction and devastation I saw on the news. I still had my children to love, my family to lean on, a sound home to live in and much for which to be grateful. For me, everything had changed but unlike them, much had remained the same. I would not forget Fukushima.

March 25, 2011

Dear Randy,

You better brush up on your geography because next week David will compete at the state level Geography Bee. It would be so fitting for him to place, given your wanderlust and association with National Geographic.

I think I need to sell your Porsche. When I see it, I am reminded of how much enjoyment and pleasure you got out of this "toy" and I wish I could keep it for the boys. It is such a beautiful car and selling it would mean I am losing another piece of you.

From a financial and practical perspective, it made all the sense in the world to sell Randy's Porsche, but I wanted the right owner for his car. It was a vintage, mint 911 that had been kept in an air-conditioned garage before Randy, so it was immaculate and beautifully preserved. However, I dreaded the thought of driving it because my experience with a manual transmission was limited to an old Volkswagen Bug from days back in Mexico. There was no comparison and I imagined Randy cringing when I attempted to shift his finely tuned machine.

March 26, 2011

Dear Randy,

Strangely enough, I think a solution to your Porsche just appeared tonight. Earlier this afternoon, Peer came over to pick up the car and deal with the potential buyers for me. As we were prepping the car, David started to polish the wheels and was excited to be with it. Peer saw this connection and later remarked he wished he had the extra cash to buy it and then sell it back to me when the boys became of age.

I asked our friend if he would be willing to house the car until the boys were ready. Even better, Peer offered to cover the expenses and maintenance—an answer to an unsaid prayer because it freed me up from the worry, while still keeping it in the family.

April 1, 2011

Dear Randy,

We went to Jacksonville for the Geography Bee. David did poorly and was crushed. He went from sad to disappointed and then from ashamed to angry. And finally, he was surly with me.

I really enjoyed our trip together and the one on one time we had. It was so much work to get there. I had to farm out Christian (he stayed with Tatiana) and Michael (with the Frazee's). It was like packing for four to go away—so many logistics and so much planning.

David had a lot of pressure because the entire school was behind him. He was the first student to ever qualify for the states. He was frustrated because he knew most of the answers, but he got the one question that flummoxed him. Anyhow, once we talked about food he cheered up.

My son was uniquely into food. He used to spend hours with my mother as she taught him to cook and bake. He had an inordinate interest in all aspects of preparing a meal— from cultivating and harvesting the ingredients to the tools that were needed in a kitchen. By the time he was 10 years old, he was into reading Robuchon's book to elevate his craft. Food was David's happy place and he found more comfort than anyone I knew in a good meal. Realizing the predisposition to addiction coursed through my son's genes, I did not want to lean on food (or any other substance) for comfort. However, at times I was thankful for this diversion because my toolbox was getting emptied and my solo-parenting challenges were many.

April 3, 2011

Dear Randy,

Michael was 10 years old today. You would have enjoyed him so much at this stage. He is more mature and controlled.

He was showing a lot of heaviness in the past few days until he told me that he was trying to forget you because the alternative of crying was too painful.

The next day he was terribly rude, and I reprimanded him. He responded with so much rage and sneaked out of the house when I gave him a time out.

I did not let Michael back inside until he apologized and chose to behave respectfully. Our cat and mouse game went on for hours until he cried his heart out and had nothing left inside. He was finally able to release his pain and was much lighter afterwards, even recognizing he felt much better after his tantrum.

This was not easy on me. At first, I was very, very angry at being disrespected. As he rebelled, I asked God to be a parent to both of us because I was losing my perspective in this new role as an only parent. I was unequivocal that his rudeness was unacceptable in our home and I locked all the doors. I figured (with a prayer) it was safe enough for him to wander around our street until he came to his senses and acknowledged that home was his safe space. I had expectations for his behavior so I also sent him to bed without dinner (but I did make him a smoothie).

Poor Michael. His relationship with Randy had been fractured. He was younger, impulsive, and energetic. With his body failing him and his health nosediving, Randy did not have the ability to handle this child with the patience Michael deserved and required. We agreed I would mostly deal with him, but Randy would participate in the easy activities like Cub Scouts, where he was not prone to mischief. Dividing and conquering worked out, even though Michael spent less time with Randy, it was mostly positive and drama free. With his father's death, not only did he lose a parent but his remaining one drastically changed. I had to become a father, and I was no longer a predictable soft landing because I was also the disciplinarian. I ran a tight ship which was new to him. I did not know if he needed to see a counselor, but Susan told me, "Some kids just shut down and won't talk to a counselor. Keep an eye on his sleeping, eating and social skills."

April 24, 2011

Dear Randy,

Peter visited and edited my portfolio. He ended up selecting about 10 images for Corbis.

Michael finally broke the school reading record with an all-time high. He set his mind to achieve this goal. Amy told me that there were tears in his eyes when he heard the announcement over the school loudspeaker.

Randy used to be an avid reader and it was commonplace for the boys to see him with a book in hand. Michael used reading as his escape, and it was also a connection to his father. To break this record meant his grades would suffer, but his teacher and I agreed this quest was a positive channel for his emotions. Reading would take his mind off of his feelings and thoughts which were overwhelming him. Breaking the Accelerated Reader school record was a big thing for a little 10-year-old boy. His feat was hugely celebrated within the St. Paul bubble. Just like his father, when Michael set his mind to accomplish a goal, he was unstoppable. I had witnessed Randy's quiet determination, so I knew that as we moved forward, I would continue to observe Michael's drive. I just had to be wise enough to properly channel him . . . and survive his persistence.

Randy had taught me a few camera settings, so I could play around for my own enjoyment. With my limited knowledge, I started to produce small shoots to keep our files active. I was astounded at how much I picked up just being around a pro, learning more than I ever imagined. Even more amazing was how much David had absorbed while he was around Randy's work. (Our kids started "working" as soon as they took their first breath). David helped me set up the lighting in the studio, adeptly connecting the equipment, knowing where to find the cables. When I asked him "How do you know where that goes?" He just remarked that he felt Dad guiding him.

I could relate to that same feeling. As I took photos, I could almost hear Randy's voice and thoughts inside my head. Although my work was pleasing, I was acutely aware I was no match to his talent and training. Nonetheless, when Peter, his production manager and closest colleague (who read Randy's eulogy), dropped in for a visit, I showed him a few of my images. It was encouraging to know that I was competent enough to embark in this direction.

The Royal Wedding of Prince William and his beautiful bride, Catherine, poignantly reminded me how far my life was from being a fairy tale. A few days later, on May 1st, Pope John Paul II was beatified. As I watched the ceremony on the news, I reminisced how Randy and I had driven 9 hours to see him when he visited Durango, Mexico. I had grown up with this traveling Pope, and I admired him and his achievements. I remember having a resonant thought, almost a prayer but not quite a formal one. "Pope John Paul, you don't have to perform another miracle to become a saint. To me, you are one already." As the Royal Wedding and beatification intersected, I had a momentary crisis of faith, some vacillation in my footing, and I needed a reminder that Heaven was real. That same night I had the most powerful visit I had ever experienced:

> *May 2, 2011*
>
> *Dear Randy*
>
> *I was having a normal night with dreams that I can't remember and then, as if the channel finally found a clear signal, you suddenly showed up in my dreams:*
>
> *You were again shirtless and young. So very handsome— your eyes were incredibly green and clear. We kissed and hugged. It felt incredibly real. I could feel your embrace and the scratchy stubbles of your beard. I did not want to kiss you because if I closed my eyes, I would lose sight of you. It was as if my senses were in conflict, each wanting to experience you and not miss a moment, but I was unable to hold on and I woke up.*

It was so real it made me cry several times today because I was reminded of how much I miss you. What a wonderful gift that was.

To say that vivid moment was a mere dream would fall short of describing what I had experienced. Only because it happened in the twilight of my sleep would it merit that description. It was not just a vision because all of my senses were engaged. I even had the awareness of trying to hold on because I knew the moment could easily dissipate. Randy's eyes were full of amusement and mischief. His hair was darker and fuller, like when he was in his late twenties. He was smiling, as if he was keeping a secret but he wanted to tell me all about it. He beckoned me to kiss him. I woke up crying when it was over because I realized this was an incredibly special experience. I yearned for another opportunity to see and feel Randy again. This "dream" sustained me for the next few months. I needed a lot of strength and courage because we would soon head to Europe for some family travel.

Scattering the Seeds
of Wanderlust

*"The world is a book and those who
do not travel read only one page."*

St. Augustine of Hippo

Randy and I were weathered travelers. We wanted our sons to navigate the globe with the ease we had developed over a lifetime of adventures. Our notion of travel embodied more than just visiting new places or being herded into organized tours. It encompassed the experience of navigating public transportation networks, making decisions on the spur of the moment (with limited information), learning to figure out how to get from point A to B while being constrained by time. We wanted them to learn how to be open to the unexpected and how to make the most out of any situation. We decided to wait until our sons were old enough to appreciate the great European cities because they were the perfect training ground.

Finally, the boys were at the right age, so I was going to show them London, Paris and Rome—only now I would be alone traveling with them to these amazing capitals. While I would make sure they saw all that was culturally relevant, Randy's unique perspective, creativity and free spirit would have complemented and augmented the experience. As a couple, we brought a balance to our travel but now, even though I would do my part, his unique worldview, and "off the wall" observations, as well as his hilarious insight would be missing. As Randy's wingman, I enjoyed following him into the unknown, but I could not afford to give into these inclinations because I had lost my partner in crime.

In fulfilling our parenting plan, I decided to start with England because one of my dear friends was living there and it was her last summer in London. As an added bonus, my brother treated our whole family to a cruise through the Mediterranean to celebrate my dad's 70th birthday. There would be much that our kids would see.

As Kim, my widow mentor had already told me, my day-to-day life was exhaustingly busy—trying to keep our ship afloat. I was so busy prior to this trip that I only heard the word "cruise" when my parents scheduled the dates. I became aware of our awesome itinerary only after we boarded the ship. Aside from England (and a few days in Paris), we would travel to Spain and Italy. A former version of me would have done extensive planning to prepare the boys for this trip. I would have checked out books, videos, and other learning material so they could appreciate the cultural landscape we were about to visit. That mother was gone, however. I could barely get us packed and I did not even know our destinations except for the airfares I had booked myself. I had become a one-man show in a three-ring circus . . . and I was also the ticket master and janitor. I had no time for the little extra's. Just staying in the game and on my feet was a real accomplishment.

Again, I journaled to stay connected with my support system. I also realized that I needed to document all that we were doing. Since Randy's death, every day was packed to the brim. I had a long list of "to-do's" that I checked off as I accomplished the mundane, the daily and the imperative.

Success was getting something done, but it was instantly relegated to the past—and I rarely looked back. I felt my memory was limited, either because my brain was too full, or the trauma of widowhood had somehow dulled my ability to remember. In another lifetime, I used to strive for excellence in anything I undertook, but since Randy's passing, I was getting very comfortable with the notion of doing a half-baked job.

6/24/2011

Dear Friends,

You are receiving this message because I am thankful our paths have crossed. As some of you may know, I have been getting ready for our trip to Europe. It was so stressful to manage the logistics—prep the house, pay the bills, pack and of course, deal with the end of the school year. I was so relieved to jump on the train to the airport and be on our way. I was rattled and excited, but barely able to cope - even if it meant undertaking such an awesome experience.

We visited Granada, Seville and Cordoba. David and Michael were in heaven with all of the Spanish chorizos, ham and olives. Africa's proximity to Spain is amazing. On a clear day you can see it across from Gibraltar. Spain's historical buildings are a mix of Moorish and later renaissance styles—sometimes grand, other times hodge-podge, occasionally bizarre, but always interesting. At Nicola's recommendation, we went to Ronda which is situated above a gorge and has a spectacular bridge that fired the boy's imagination with ideas of bungee jumping.

By far, Christian was my biggest surprise, walking more than his full measure and keeping up with our pace like a little trouper. He loved the churches and asked me countless times to re-tell the story of why Jesus was on a cross. The thorn crown was particularly interesting as were the bleeding knees. All of the paintings and sculptures in the cathedrals fascinated him and I can see why religious art was so important to educate the illiterate which at age 4, he is!

The first leg of our trip we visited some old friends from the Venezuela days. He was the principal of my brother's high school and my dad had also been on that Board of Directors. In an unfortunate twist of fate, his wife Maria Luisa, had been widowed when she was around my age and left with four young children (ages 6-13). Manolo was her second husband and helped her raise her kids. Even though our circumstances were different, we obviously shared a closeness that could not be described in words. I was immediately comfortable to be in her company.

A week later we all boarded the cruise. Everyone had a great time. Michael loved running up the stairs and doing rock climbing. David enjoyed the freedom of the tween activities and independence of roaming around without supervision. He would stay out until 11:00 PM. I don't know how I am going to cope with the teenage years. Christian loved the shows which were really good. We saw the ice-skating and he was squealing with delight and clapping all of the time. It was so cute. He would scream when the skaters did their tricks. The food was delicious and so hard to limit the portions. It was a great way for our family to spend time together and celebrate my dad's birthday.

I was incredibly blessed to have the opportunity and means to travel with the boys. Given our new reality, showing the boys this part of the world was a stretch on my budget and my brothers generosity was a huge help. Nonetheless, I could not help but reflect that this was not what Randy and I would have planned. One way was not better than the other—just different.

6/27/2011

Dear Friends and Family,

First of all— please don't feel obligated to respond to my litany. E-mail is such an efficient way to journal. Otherwise I'd forget these details of our experiences.

We boarded the cruise in Malaga. Our first stop was Valencia which was unexciting except for the fact that I met up with Beatriz, my best friend from grade school. She left Venezuela when we were both 14 years old. Our friendship is still as special as when we were little girls—time and life have not made a dent.

Our second stop was . . . ROME! Despite my many visits, the beauty of that city never fails to amaze me. No matter where you set your eyes, there are stunning buildings to gaze upon. We woke up really early to catch the train into St. Peter's. The cruise tours are very costly. Since my brother knew how to get around, we opted to "wing" it and do it all ourselves, leaving Christian behind with my parents. The older boys got to see St. Peter's Basilica, the Coliseum, the Spanish Steps, eat a gelato by the Trevi Fountain and toss a coin over the backs to make sure they would return again. All in the span of 8 hours, we walked and walked and walked!!! The real adventure was getting back to the ship on time. We barely made it. We had to run, run, run. It was NOT for the faint of heart. Our downfall was that the returning train was late, and we left from a different station. We almost missed the boat.

In Florence the boys saw the Ponte Vecchio and we climbed
to the top of the Duomo. It was a real thrill and again, we
got our cardio work-out to burn all of the calories we were
consuming! It's such a beautiful city. It's amazing what one
family with power and money can patronize: the cradle of
the Renaissance. We located a little apothecary that has
been in existence since the 1200's. They exported their
medicinal formulas around the world, including France,
through Catherine de Medici when she became Queen. One
of the makers traveled with her and later named his creation
"Cologne" (after the city). And so, perfume was born. This
apothecary is still up and running but you have to be "in the
know" because it is in a non-descript location. The formulas
are centuries old and their customers were all kings, queens,
and nobles . . . fascinating.

Since my brother rented a car, we were more in control of our
destiny and upon returning to Livorno, the port, we detoured
and quickly saw the leaning tower of Pisa. Quickly may not
accurately describe the dash that the boys and I made to snap
a photo while Gene circled around and waited for us in the
car. Another workout.

The final stop was the island of Corsica, the birth- place of
Napoleon. I did not get to see much but David did go into his
home. Corsica is laden with natural beauty. It is probably one
of the most incredible places in the world. Amazingly, it has
both stunning coves and ski resorts in the high mountains. A
much bigger island than one would imagine.

Well, that concludes the amazing Mediterranean Cruise
and Italy 101 for David and Michael. I am so thankful that

Gene made this trip possible for us because it was a totally unexpected and wonderful experience. I just hope that the boys remember all of the trekking we did.

We said goodbye to my family, and I set off for England with David and Michael. Christian would remain with my parents and their friends, allowing me the flexibility to travel without having to look out for a small child. Even though Michael and David were older, it was daunting to be the only adult in charge on foreign soil.

7/2/2011

Dear Friends and Family,

Who ever said that London had grey, dreary skies? It must be the Seattle conspirators. The boys will remember mild, cool, blue skies and a little rain shower once in a while—no big deal! They might recall the heat of one day (the hottest of the year), worse than Florida—but overall, it will be a great impression of wonderful English weather!!!

We left Christian with my parents in Spain and headed to London on June 18th, Randy's birthday. I think it was fitting to travel in the same day by ship, car, train, airplane and bus. It was a true tribute to Randy because his life was mostly defined by his travel. Our trip was smooth and miraculously I found my way to Carolina's home with these simple directions: from Stanstead airport get on the bus to Lord Cricket's Ground, cross the park, look for Carluccio's on the corner. My flat is on the first floor. It seemed almost incredible to do that exactly and as we crossed the street, she was waving at us from the window! It was too easy!

219

We stayed with Caro, another friend who dated from the Venezuela years. She and I happened to coincide in South Florida when we were in our early 20's. A long time ago, when Randy transitioned from travel to people photography, she was his first model. Her hospitality allowed us to a home base and from there we explored city. I also felt at ease with the company of another mother. We stayed in London long enough for the boys to learn how to navigate the Tube and use public transportation.

We climbed St. Paul's dome which is beautiful and pristine since they just had THE WEDDING (photos are all over the place). The genius of Christopher Wren was to build a huge dome that dominated the skyline from the outside. Housed within the big dome, he built an interior one that was much lower and allowed the congregation to gaze at the fantastic ceiling frescoes because the paintings were close enough to be properly appreciated.

The interior is simply beautiful and what impressed me the most was the chapel behind the main altar which is completely dedicated to the 28,000 Americans that lost their lives in WW2. The stained-glass windows have motifs for every state of the Union and they keep a book with all the names of the fallen soldiers.

Throughout our visit in London, there were many visible reminders of the appreciation Britain had for the US intervention in that war. Michael has really taken to climbing these domes and loves the height and view they afford. He just sprints up the steps as if they are nothing. David and I will not forget the cardio-workout we did with all of this climbing.

After St. Paul we walked to the British Museum which keeps the Rosetta Stone, mummies and many other strange objects. Our second day was ALL day at the Tower which was fascinating to me since I'm interested in English history. The boys were keen on seeing the fabulous Crown Jewels and listening to the Beefeaters (guards) entertain with colorful anecdotes of mysteries, murders and executions—totally boy stuff. We also went to the Science, Natural History and Royal Air Force Museums where we met an actual pilot that was in the 2nd World War, including the War Cabinet Rooms from which Churchill led Britain.

For a few days, we were lucky to have Gene join us before he returned back to Mexico. We also found tickets to Wicked, the prequel to the Wizard of Oz. We had to do the London theater. It was an amazing production. Most striking was how the story cleverly wove into the Oz tale. It was helpful viewing the movie the night before, so it all made sense. If you enjoy theater, this is "a must." I am still thinking about it.

We also visited Westminster Abbey and saw the graves of many notables. They offer a "scavenger" hunt that earned the boys a huge chocolate coin, making it totally worth their while to read all of the epitaphs and other markings around the church. That same day we RAN to see the Changing of Guards. In the course of this sprint, I lost the boys for the 45-minute ceremony. It was so crowded and packed. By the time I reached the area, they were nowhere to be seen. While I was slightly panicky, I figured I'd find them after it was all over. Fortunately, they stuck together because they remembered my "what to do if you are lost" instructions. They actually spotted me from a high point where they had placed

*themselves on the gate. Both David and Michael concluded
that I was the one who was lost and not them!*

In addition to all that we did in London, I took the boys on a side trip to Bath and Stonehenge. It was a bit of work to figure out how to get there and where to stay. Arriving at a new city, disoriented, and with two youngsters was nerve wracking. Fortunately, after walking around a bit, I found a visitor information office that pointed us in the right direction.

Even though Bath was a charming city with some very old Roman Baths (hence the name), we would remember this colorful incident of our visit there. Walking alongside the river, I suddenly felt as if a shower of hail rained upon me with loud cracks popping all around. At the same time, my face was wet and as I wiped my cheeks, my hands were covered with a muddy gooey substance. Much to my dismay, I realized that I was pooped-on by passing seagulls. Thank goodness my mouth was closed! It was so disgusting, smelly and gross. I was distressed when my beautiful Etcetera coat got stained with bird shit. Meanwhile, the boys (who flanked each of my sides) were unscathed. Clearly, I was the chosen one. Thankfully, there was a restaurant nearby where I spent the better part of 20 minutes washing-up. I stood by the quality of my line of clothes because the coat cleaned off really well. After it was all done, we counted the "missiles" that landed where I was standing. I got hit by 4, but there were about 25 on the ground. They say these birds actually aim at their "target" and it is good luck to get bombed. Yeah, right!

*Stonehenge. The big deal about this monolith is why? Why
would anyone undertake the monumental task of moving
SUV+ sized rocks through a thick forest for about 200 miles to
this particular place—more than 5000 years ago? And it seems
that this location was still considered special even 10000 years
ago because there are visible signs of a prior circle, made by*

even earlier people. On this same side-trip, we also saw the
Salisbury Cathedral, home to one of the four existing Magna
Carta documents (and it has the best preserved one). This very
historical document was the base of many other important
ones that would follow (American Revolution, French
Revolution, etc.). David was really into this—Michael, not so
much.

Thus, this concludes our England section. I feel we saw a lot,
but there was so much more we could have done. I am so
appreciative of Carolina's hospitality because it would have
not been possible to do it otherwise. London is very pricey.
Everything looks like the same cost as the US except for the
fact that you need to add sixty percent more to the tag. They
must find the U.S. to be a bargain! We did much because I
kept the boys at a rapid pace. On our way to the Tube we
grabbed sandwiches at the local grocery, so we could eat on
the run. The weather helped in allowing us to make the most
of the day which was pretty long since it gets dark around
10pm. Next stop: Paris and then HOME!

When we stepped off the Chunnel and got to Paris, I did not feel the
former apprehension I had experienced upon arriving to a new city. I had
been to Paris. It had been a few years since my last visit, but I knew the
lay of the land which made a huge difference to my nerves. Nonetheless,
the city had changed a lot and what I remembered as charming then,
now looked run-down—including the hotel that I booked for our stay.
The chic and bohemian Montmartre of my memory was in reality
disappointingly shoddy and dilapidated. All my OCD triggers started
alarming at the same time. After a momentary meltdown, we all took a
collective deep breath and made the best out of our accommodations.

Finding an alternative at a late hour, with the rain, lugging a big suitcase and having two little boys in tow was just not going to happen.

Even though we visited all of the requisite sights and climbed to the top of the Eiffel tower (more cardio), there was one indelible memory of Paris that would be the most remarkable one. Walking down the Champs-Elysees we saw this wild man waving at us with manic fervor. It was one of those moments where the scene in front could not register because his face did not match the place. We had no expectations of coinciding with anyone, but much to our astonishment, the wild man was Dr. Krempler—the school principal. He and his wife were celebrating their anniversary in Paris. It was their first overseas trip. They were just as stunned to have spotted us. It was incredible to come together. . . across the big pond. It was a good reminder to me that while I did not have a partner, I would always find friendly faces—even in faraway places.

Returning home to the lazy, sultry, Florida summer offered a much welcome rest from our forays and European adventure. I felt blessed to have made such a trip, grateful for all the help along the way, and incredibly proud to have pulled it off. It was a relief to start preparing for the next school year and slip back into a much-welcomed routine.

As I bathed Christian, every so often I reminded him how much his father used to enjoy putting him to bed. Randy was impressed that Christian would "clean-up" the tub on his own and he did not squirm or squiggle when he was dressing him in his jammies.

August 2011,

Dear Randy,

As Christian caught sight of the Ft. Lauderdale airport, a certain view must have triggered his memory because he said,

"This is Daddy's airport." A few nights later, as I was tucking him into bed, he became sad and teary-eyed. He told me, "I don't know why I am sad but I am." When I asked him if he missed you, he replied, "Mom, we are all alone." I told him not to worry because you were in his heart and that we had been able to manage in spite of your not being with us. A few days later he remarked again how he was thinking of you, so I went to your closet and let him smell your shirt.

Christian finally understood that his father would not be coming back from Heaven. It was a heavy moment for me to realize that he had finally become aware of his reality. He was just a little over four years old. He was a sweet soul and he was such a comfort to me. I was saddened that Randy would miss knowing this delightful child and in turn Christian would never experience his father.

As I walked through our house and enjoyed the space we created, I could only be thankful for all that Randy taught me—for his insights and for his desire to please me. We had undergone a huge remodel a few years before Christian's birth, and I was incredibly grateful for the home Randy built for us. We had our love story. I then remembered Lee Anne's words when we wrote Randy's eulogy: At least I had known how it felt to be truly loved by my husband.

Embracing the
Notion of Change

"A widow who is all alone, with no one to take care of her,
has placed her hope in God and continues to pray
and ask him for his help night and day."

1 Timothy 5:5 (GNT)

"The Lord has a special place in his heart for widows and orphans." I met Catherine at an event honoring her. Upon our introduction, she uttered these words which reflected what I had already begun to experience. Soon after, she invited me to be a panelist on one of her seminars where I would tell the story of my widowhood in front of a live audience. When I worked at Baxter, I used to deliver the opening or closing of large conferences, and as a board President, I also had chaired a plethora of events and had given many speeches.

But that seemed like a lifetime ago, and I was unsure I could ever get on a stage again. To deliberately relive my tragedy out loud seemed like a nerve-wracking thought. It had been a little over 18 months since Randy had died and I had not considered having a story to tell, much less that it could be inspirational.

I imagined being in front of an audience would exert an emotional toll, so I was filled with apprehension, and yet I felt compelled to say yes. I explained to the boys that I would tell what happened to our family and expressed my nervousness. They wanted to know why I would agree to do that, and my response was, "Because I'm sure it will help someone else. So please say a prayer for your mother."

At the end of the seminar, two women approached me. With tears in their eyes, they thanked me profusely for the hope and strength I had given them. One was the sister, and the other was the wife of a man who had passed . . . on December 31, 2011. It was the same date as Randy's death, but one year later. This was an odd coincidence that surprised us, yet it connected the three of us. I had no doubt that my courage to speak would impact someone in the audience, but I never expected to know who that might be or share a significant date with them. This seemingly small synchronicity confirmed that my willingness to be open would in turn confer grace upon me.

September 2011

Dear Randy,

I landed the book translation job. The Lord is so merciful and kind because His timing was impeccable and His graciousness vast. I am thrilled at the work and for the money. It will resolve a lot of issues and I will be able to do more with the boys. By the way, I need help with Michael. He is having trouble managing his emotions.

Over the summer, Christian's godfather connected me with a medical publishing house for some translation work. Because of my healthcare background, the terms were familiar, and the work was interesting. My initial work was to write the copy for brochures but soon after I got an offer to translate an "Introduction to Nursing" textbook. The pay was great but more importantly, I remained in control of my schedule (or so I thought) and I could continue working from home. The assignment turned out to be a huge challenge. From the onset, it was emotionally draining because the first chapter was all about cardiovascular nursing. As I read the words describing Randy's symptoms, I was reminded of how clueless we were about his health. In hindsight, his tiredness, pallor, palpitations, and anxiety were all related to heart disease. Randy and I had been ignorant, and worse yet, his doctors were arrogantly dismissive and terribly misguided.

Adding to the emotional difficulty, I was working on texts from an Indian physician. Clearly, English was not his first language, so his writing was confusing. Translating this book was tough—more work than I had ever imagined— and I had to keep late hours to meet the deadlines. More than once I was tempted to walk away but I did not want to tarnish my family connection, so in my decision I was caught "between a rock and a hard place."

Thanksgiving 2011

Dear Randy,

We've been on a cruise with your family and will celebrate Thanksgiving with them. The kids had a good time and for me it was a rest from that chaotic translation job.

In the end, I delivered on time and earned a significant bonus for my expediency. As life returned to its normal cadence, I remember feeling grateful to fold laundry—a never-ending task that most mothers would rather eschew. For weeks, piles of clean clothes languished in the basket because I was so overextended. Even though translating allowed me to set my own hours and work from home, I learned the hard way to be wary of my commitments. It was a reminder that life continued to be a

229

delicate balancing act.

> *Christmas 2011*
>
> *Dear Randy,*
>
> *We had a good Christmas. I had a minor surgery on the 19th. Did you come to keep me company while the anesthesia was wearing off? I woke up to an empty house, silent except for the noise of you plopping onto the couch. As I was in a semi-conscious state, I reasoned that it had to be the wood was expanding until I heard the noise for the third time and figured it was you.*
>
> *I thought you would come during Christmas, but you have not, and I don't remember any of my dreams.*

Several years ago, we went to the home of the Vice-Consul of Taiwan in Panama. They were moving to Uruguay and were selling their furniture. Randy fell in love with a family room set which cost more to ship to the US than its selling price. It had a beautiful wood frame with thin removable cushions designed for comfort in the hot tropical months. When Randy sat, he "plopped" on the sofa at the end of the day, looking forward to some relaxing TV time.

The minor surgery was not an emergency, but it seemed like one because I had just a couple of days to prepare (my doctor suggested to schedule the surgery before the end of the year for insurance reimbursement purposes). After I was discharged, Lee Anne brought me home and made sure I was sleeping comfortably before she left. According to the doctor, I would be up and ready in time to receive the kids after school. It was mid-morning as I drifted in and out of consciousness. While the anesthesia wore off, I heard creaks that broke the silence and they sounded just like when Randy slumped into the Taiwanese couch. The house was empty and at first, I tried to reason the origin of the noise. Eventually it occurred to me that perhaps Randy was watching over me . . . which gave me comfort and allowed me to drift back to a sound sleep. When I woke up, I reflected on the sounds I heard. It was another reminder that somehow, I was not alone, and someone was looking out for me.

Again, I did not send out Christmas cards. Instead, I ended up waiting until Easter which became my new tradition. The two older boys made sure Christian fully experienced Santa's visit this year. They made it all so real for him—even picking up the phone to "call" Santa when Christian started to misbehave. The little guy enjoyed the season so going through the motions was even more meaningful: gingerbread houses, a manger, and letting him decorate the lower third of the tree that year. Once again, it looked gaudy as every single ornament he was able to hang was dangling from the branches. It was now Christian's turn to be excited. His favorite gifts were Peter Pumpkin—the hamster that Michael bought for him (care and cage cleaning included in the deal) and a little bike that David assembled.

When we thought we were done with opening presents, the boys discovered a whole other PILE at our front door. For the third year in a row, we were surprised at the thoughtfulness of our Secret Santa. Christian was thrilled because the one present on his list he did not get was a cargo truck that could hold other little cars. Incredibly, such a truck was among the doorstep gifts!

The boys were doing very well, and I had mixed emotions realizing that I seemed to be the only one missing Randy. I assumed that was healthy for the kids and one less concern for me as a mom. Other than lighting of some firecrackers with messages to Heaven, we did not do much else. Christmas was filled with blessings that came wrapped in many shapes and colors, but they all were packaged with a great measure of love, care and concern. With God's grace, I was getting through life and I hoped one day the boys would realize all they had in spite of their loss.

As we entered 2012, there was much doomsday speculation because the Mayan Calendar prophesied the end of times that December. I did not pay much attention to this notion partly because as Catholics, "only the Father" knows the day and time (Mathew 24:36). In addition, I remember not caring one way or the other because my feet were planted on Earth, but my soul longed for Heaven. I had lost any fear of dying because it meant reuniting with Randy. I was compelled when I started reading the complicated book of Revelation. It was not easy reading, but it was fascinating. Since my world had pretty much ended as I knew it, I was keenly interested in these writings—even though they were hard to understand.

I continued on my journey to learn as much as I could about Heaven and the afterlife, choosing to keep within the boundaries of Christianity because I wanted to remain within my comfort zone. I joined BSF (Bible Study Fellowship) to further study the book of Revelation. For the laity, this was the most in depth and demanding non-denominational Bible Study available where I lived. It required a high level of commitment for anyone seeking to learn without the reward of a certificate or degree. I was fascinated by the subject and had decided to get some more formal knowledge, adding to what I had already absorbed from the books that came into my life. I continued to be curious about life after death and avidly read many accounts of near-death experiences (NDE's). I felt that I was researching the next adventure and getting to know the lay of the land.

A few months later, we woke up to a small family misfortune. Christian's two-month old hamster had died in his sleep, allowing Christian to experience death in a more tangible way.

February 2012,

Dear Randy,

Peter Pumpkin just died. We had a little funeral for Christian's benefit. He hopes his hamster goes to "people Heaven", so he can be with you and Christian can see him when he goes to Heaven. We had this conversation:

- "Daddy wanted to die."

- "No, I don't think he did. I think he would have wanted to see you grow up."

- "But he can see me from Heaven."

- "Yes, but he would have wanted to talk to you."

- "We can talk when we pray."

- "Yes, but he would have wanted to give you a hug and enjoy you in person."

- "He can enjoy me when I sleep. Daddy is with Jesus."

After this conversation, I wondered—Does Christian know all of this just because he came this way? I cannot have influenced him this much.

Life finally turned into to a predictable ebb and flow of the tides. I was no longer confronting unexpected storms, flash floods or devastating tsunamis. Nonetheless with three growing kids, my day to day was far from placid and there was always something going on or vying for my attention. I had learned how to keep the paddle board from flipping over and was actually moving forward with the support of my social network. My friends, neighbors and even new acquaintances continued to help me with the boys, providing friendship and company.

As a fashion consultant for Etcetera, I had grown my agency

to a respectable size, but I was still a small fish in the pond. When a significantly larger business was about to change hands, the owner freely handed me her client list. It was sales growth on a silver platter. Sort of. Her clients had not been contacted for the better part of a year, and the list had not been updated, so sales had languished.

I felt awkward calling new clients to explain the change of ownership, but I plodded through and integrated. I was incredibly grateful because higher sales allowed me to remain a stay-at-home parent which my boys required more than ever. "Mom, don't ever tell anyone that I'm helping you with the clothes," David and Michael pleaded as we unpacked, buttoned up or hung the garments. I suppose they would have been mortified if their friends caught wind that they were hanging ladies' clothes. "This is now the family business, and there is no shame in helping me." I reminded them that my earnings went towards supporting our household expenses and we needed to be grateful. David was still able to recall my corporate days—the travel, and my absences. He would tell his brother, "Michael, you DON'T want Mom going back to Baxter."

Summer 2012

Dear Randy,

Having done Europe, Park City and the cruise with your parents, we are going to stay put this summer. Between Junior Lifeguards, the pool and tons of invitations to the Club, I think we just need to lay low.

In February I landed a new addition to my ETC agency and it has been a lot of work to integrate. In June I started to work out at a new gym with Dorothy and it was tough. I could not walk normally for days. She has an au-pair who can watch Christian while we exercise. I have an incredible connection with Dot, my new friend.

*I also sold your Porsche. It was easy to sell but hard to see it
go. However, that money finished paying off the house.*

A sudden buyer showed up for Randy's Porsche. I had a hard decision
to make because once again, this transported me to the "letting go" stage.
David was only thirteen years old and it would be a long while before I
could allow him drive Randy's fourth baby. I realized if I sold the Porsche
and cashed in some of our Apple shares, I could finish paying off our
mortgage. It probably made more financial sense to keep the stock and
write off the interest, but securing our homestead gave me a peace of
mind that was priceless. The boys and I said our goodbyes to Randy's car
with a final joyride, some last photos. Then I shut my eyes and did not
look back.

After two years and a half of being a widow, I was finally at ease with
my new identity, coming to terms with what was not and all that had
changed. It took a long while to comfortably acknowledge and accept I
was indeed that "poor woman,"—an only parent who no longer shared
a life with her husband. This loss stung the most when I faced either a
parenting challenge or a moment of pride because someone who was
equally vested in our children was missing. A moment of difficulty or a
successful accomplishment were both equally poignant. My losses were
somewhat mitigated seeing the boys thrive, knowing I survived, and
having the certainty that no matter how bad things seemed, I could cling
on to the faith that had sustained me through the turmoil.

I carried myself with the confidence of a woman who has already
experienced her worse nightmare. Barring a terminal illness or harm
befalling one of my kids, I could not imagine anything more devastating
than what I had experienced. Having lived through fear, anxiety,

and trauma—I felt anything else that life threw at me would pale in comparison. Walking through the fire, I came out at the other end refined and liberated.

On a social level, letting people know I was a widow was not easy. In the beginning, I was surrounded by the protective cocoon of the St. Paul community and EVERYONE knew what had happened, so I did not have to explain. It was relatively easy to attend social functions alone because even before Randy's death, I was on my own. His prolonged work absences were familiar to everyone who knew us, so this was not a new situation that I had to embrace. The vast majority of my friends were married, and I was blessed they continued to socially include me. Some women experience isolation when former couple-friends distance themselves after a change in their marital status. I was grateful to have an ample social network that provided an escape to the doldrums of being an only parent. As I moved forward, my circle widened including new friends who were also on a fresh start after a divorce. I could see the shock in their eyes and sense their abashment when they learned I was a widow. Even though I felt ancient, I did not look the part, so many were surprised. I had to learn to gently allay their discomfort.

Christmas 2012

Dear Randy,

I broke sales records with the Fall and Holiday collection, placing in the top 20% of the country.

Most absorbing had been the planning and execution of the Fashion Show. I am leading an amazingly capable team with Sue and Renee as co-chairs. We are a trifecta, complementing each other incredibly well. It is easy for me because I'm mostly in charge of the overall management.

I was on the cusp of becoming one of the top consultants in South Florida and occasionally, of the country. I did some heavy lifting but was aware my success was the godsend of "inheriting" two agencies. The first one gave me a base start and I learned some new skills. When I landed the second client list, I was poised to grow. Some would call this fortuitous luck, but I knew I was blessed. It is just one of the many lifelines I received to help me navigate the uncharted waters ahead.

I had the reputation of being an unflappable leader who could make the big events happen, but I did not think my nerves (and limited time) were up to chairing another fundraiser for St. Paul. I thought I left those days behind, but this was the Fashion Show—a complex event that raised the Christmas bonuses for the faculty and staff.

As an eight-grader, David was graduating from middle school. His class would walk the runway in formal wear, a rite of passage that signaled their time in this cocoon was ending. There were many willing to help but someone with the courage (or insanity) had to step up to lead . . . and everyone wanted me to be that person.

There was little elasticity left in my rubber band, so I was very hesitant to take the reins. I eventually acquiesced, knowing this could be my "Thank You" to St. Paul's faculty for all their support after Randy's death. With the help of my co-chairs, the Fashion Show was a brilliant and successful event. Not surprisingly, our numbers surpassed the fundraising targets by a long mile. Previously, I would have been elated and felt a sense of accomplishment along with a good measure of pride. Now, I was just thankful to have pulled it off without a hitch. What used to feel good to me had vastly changed and all I aspired was to move on and check it off my list.

As Christmas approached, I reflected on our third year without

Randy. It was evident we were doing pretty well —even better than I could have ever anticipated. I conscientiously chose to avoid thinking how life might have been had Randy overcome his health issues. Neither did I dwell on how we could both have imploded had he been alive but unhealthy. Living in the past or the unrealized future was irrelevant. I chose to live in the present moment. Even though there was much missing in our lives, I felt that we were being looked after and were blessed. It could have been much worse.

I chose to totally trust God, but I was still learning how to break the old habits of being Debbie—of trying to be in control, thinking I could determine our future by sheer will and hard work. After three years, I could look back to see how God had been at my side through the thick quagmire, raising me when I thought I could no longer breathe, and letting me know in the small and big ways that He would unequivocally take care of us. Mine was not a blind trust and the Lord certainly did not have to earn it. He had always been there for me. I just had to open my soul wide enough to experience His mercy, patience, and love. In doing so, I found a welcome release from the claws of anxiety and the all-corroding grip of fear.

Policies and Philosophies

"Look at the birds: they do not plant seeds, gather a harvest and put it in barns; yet your Father in heaven takes care of them! Aren't you worth much more than birds?"

Matthew 6:26 (GNT)

December 2014

Dear Randy,

This year you have been absent. This one has been the most difficult, except for year one. I started writing about your passing but did not finish the manuscript. The story of our love could be a second book as well. We were special, epic with all our lows and highs. I don't think I can ever love that way again.

My biggest question is why did it all have to be so hard and so intense? It's like we crammed a lifetime of living into twenty years. From our engagement, to our marriage, to your death. Why was it so hard on me and what am I supposed to do with all of this?

After Randy died, I used to refer to my life as a novel, feeling I had become the lead character in an unwanted saga. It was simply a metaphor that seemed appropriate given my circumstances.

Once the initial traumatic months had passed, life clamored at my heels and I had to face the daunting task of being the only parent. Rising from the ashes to build what would be our family's new life, I became incredibly focused on keeping us moving forward. There were sporadic moments when I jumped off the hamster wheel, but realistically, I had little time to ruminate over major existential questions. However, upon nearing the four-year widowhood mark, I found myself back to pondering the "Why" question.

Randy and I had moved mountains to marry. We overcame alcoholism and prescription drug addiction. Our family was young. After all of the blows, we emerged stronger than ever as a couple, I thought we were ironclad. It was like we had finally reached the summit and before being able to fully savor victory, Randy was gone. I was mired in the feeling of having this vast trove of knowledge which was attained at a great personal cost and sacrifice. There had to be a way that I could pay it forward, that I could lessen the pain for the next person, or that I could somehow scatter my nuggets of wisdom so the insight into my grief could benefit another shattered soul.

I never expected to actually publish all that had happened to me, to Randy, to us. Because writing was therapeutic, I penned my most personal thoughts and feelings during the worst time of my life. As life progressed and unfolded, healing came in different ways and I shelved my journals. Nevertheless, in retrospect there were a few "signs" that pointed towards this path of writing a book and becoming a reluctant author.

The first one popped up decades ago, in Mexico, when I was wrapping up my senior year in college. Soon-to-be engineers had to enroll in a mandatory communications course meant to "round off" our technical education. My male friends were looking forward to the vivaciously attractive girls who were majoring in Communications. We arrogantly assumed the class would be a breeze as compared to all our math, statistics and sciences coursework.

It was not as easy as we had imagined. Writing papers about our thoughts, abstractions, and other esoteric matters was challenging to the engineering mind. We were used to the tangible and measurable, to the notion of cause and effect. However, I found enjoyment in doing the homework. It was like a new door had opened and I was peering into an unknown realm. Our communications teacher was in her early twenties, funny, animated, and she was relatable. As she graded our assignments, she cajoled a few of us to participate in a national writing contest. Since my essay was already done, I agreed to her request, submitted my paper, and then forgot all about it.

"Class, I have a great announcement ... and some not so good news to share with you," she explained several weeks later. "In this room we have the grand winner of the national contest." There was palpable suspense in the air as we wondered who it might be. "The bad news is ... this is a Communications class and none of you majoring in this field is that person. Instead, one of the engineers won the contest." To my astonishment, I had been selected as the first-place recipient in all of Mexico. While my professor was dismayed that the winner was not in her department, she was very encouraging. She said to me, "Deborah, you have talent and must continue to write."

No one had ever told me I was a good writer, and the sign for me was winning first place in the entire country. I called my parents and said with elation: "Can you believe I won a national essay contest? Do you think I should go to graduate school and study journalism?" My mom, who was always open to the unconventional, was encouraging. I think my father was mildly shocked but did not shoot down my idea. However, I tried

241

but was unable to reconcile this newfound horizon with my Engineering degree. After the initial euphoria, reason prevailed. The practical and pragmatic voice in my head thwarted this fledgling aspiration before it even had a chance to fully form as a coherent thought.

I pursued an MBA, which was much more aligned and complimentary career-wise. For many years, my writing was limited to business proposals and executive summaries. When Randy got sick and after his death, I recorded my thoughts, feelings and activity in long emails or I journaled in my diary. As time went by, my entries became sparser, evidence that I had come to terms with my loss. The boys were growing older, so I was pulled into all sorts of directions. Time was my most precious resource and my need to live in the present overshadowed the respite I received when I poured my soul onto a piece of paper. I stored my journal and I stopped writing with regularity.

The second sign occurred when my friend Nick unexpectedly reached out via email. He lived in Singapore and found me while updating his wife's contact list. Both Nick and Joyce had mentored me when I was a very inexperienced newcomer at Baxter Healthcare. She was a capable, collected and super smart lady who always offered the perfect words of wisdom. We lost track of each other when I stopped sending out Christmas cards and they moved to the Far East.

Nick wrote: "Deb, I'm going to send you a longer email. When you read it, sit down." Three months prior, lovely and wise Joyce had succumbed to pancreatic cancer. As I read his message, waves of sadness coursed through my body as I thought about what he and his three kids were going through. I wrote back. "Nick, when you read my email, you take a seat as well. We share more than you can imagine." He had no idea that Randy had died.

As the division head of a global company, I surmised Nick had a wide network of acquaintances. However, I was the only person in his circle that could relate to his new circumstances and to his unfortunate reality as the remaining parent. Nick needed to talk to me. It was not easy to coordinate our schedules for a conversation. Singapore is twelve hours ahead of EST, but I knew my empathy would help him navigate the very bumpy road ahead. As I mentally prepared for our phone call, I realized we were emotionally in very different places. His loss was recent while I had four years under my belt. My journey had evolved day by day and ever so slowly. I could look back on my progress on a daily, weekly and finally on a monthly basis. That first year was traumatic. I could not recall what or when it happened. It must be a basic survival skill not to remember pain once it has passed. To effectively help my friend, however, I had to return to the early months in my grief journey and re-inhabit the space that no one wants to relive. How could I go back there? I realized that the contents in my journal could deliver me right to where he was, month three.

Nick and I spoke a few times, and he was profusely grateful we had connected. Early on, the mentoring I received was comforting and helpful. Now I could repay it for another. I saw that my letters to Randy contained valuable insight into the grief process. Moreover, there was a community in California with a situation similar to mine and one of my friends asked, "Can I share your emails? Your writing would help my friend understand how to help and give her some insight". At one time or another, many had encouraged me to write a book, telling me that my story was inspiring. Between my journal, emails and the letters, I realized that I had documented the evolution of being an out of season widow.

The third sign was meeting the publishers of Chicken Soup for the Soul a few months after I reconnected with Nick. I surmised the Lord had put this new acquaintance in my path for a good reason. However, once I talked to an editor, her feedback was not supportive of my "Dear Randy" format. She suggested I take some writing classes and present it differently. The task was too formidable at a time when my sons were just entering the throes of adolescence. Navigating male puberty was decimating and definitely not the time to entertain a new challenge. Nonetheless, the seed was planted and the notion of writing my story remained an aspiration that languished on the shelves of my mind until the time was right.

Sadly, because of cancer and other diseases, the number of younger than expected widows is increasing at a pace unseen in prior generations. I hope my experiences in *Beyond the Breakpoint* provide insights on how a great loss feels on a granular level, so the caring friend or relative may be more effective in supporting a loved one through this difficult journey. For those who have experienced a major loss, including a divorce, layoff or another life altering change, this book could also provide a window of hope and empathy. Along the way, I also developed a few policies and philosophies that helped me forge ahead which I would like to share.

Because of my vulnerability and openness, many people have confided anecdotes or experiences that were special or extraordinary to them. Some might be unexpected butterflies or an uncommon bird showing up on their window sill. Others find pennies in unusual places, coined on a significant year. They might come across mundane objects that convey a deeply personal meaning to the living, reminding them of their deceased. Other examples are "coincidences", small miracles or signs. People usually do not divulge these personal stories because there is no scientific or logical explanation, and no one wants to be seen as kooky or weird.

In this book I have shared a few of my own experiences where I felt

244

the presence of Randy such as the light switches clacking loudly or my dream state visits. I've had many "coincidences" that pepper my life, so I have no doubt that somehow our loved ones are able to look after us. We just have to be sufficiently open to interpret the signs and acknowledge the help. Pay attention to your dreams. Aside from the experience when I had the surgery and the vivid dream almost one year prior, Randy did not ever come back to me in those sensorial, tangible ways. However, there were many instances, too many to recount, where I knew that he, God or the angels had intervened.

The most memorable one of these was on June 10, 2017. On this day, we would have celebrated twenty-two years of marriage. I remember waking up and saying to Randy, "Gosh, it must be nice to be perched up there and just watch me do all the heavy lifting from the comfort of your cloud." I was not angry or bitter, just stating a fact since my hands were full, dealing with Michael and his wild adolescence.

That same evening, about 9:00 p.m., I got the call no parent wants to receive. Michael was at a Bethesda Hospital in Delray. He was fine but had been in a car accident. Nine kids had climbed into an SUV and, in a moment of distraction, the car was T-boned at an intersection. I drove up to the hospital, knowing that Michael was unharmed, but my hands were trembling and my nerves were frayed.

As I merged onto I-95, I said to Randy, "I take that back. You really were hard at work today. Thank God, Michael is okay." Walking into the ER and meeting all the parents was surreal. We could have easily been at a party because so many families knew each other. Instead, we had congregated in the cold, sterile and chaotic pediatric ward to pick up our very much alive children who should have been seriously injured or even dead. Everyone said it was a miracle no one was permanently maimed. Only one girl had a fractured bone. Someone remarked "An angel must have been looking out for these teens." I knew that angel by name.

More than a decade has passed since Randy's death. It is my joy and satisfaction to have ushered my older sons onto their adulthood path. They are grown and flown. It was not easy meeting each child where they were in their own grief journey. Each one had their unique situation to deal with, including me. We remain open to counseling because mourning for my sons will continue as they reach new milestones such as their graduation, their wedding, or their first child.

I still mourn, but my future does not hold such momentous occasions because my horizon is wider. Nonetheless, whenever we reach a new big milestone (like going away to college) I still revisit my loss with sadness. For my children's sake, in the early years I cried alone at night. I repressed some of my emotions because I thought it was the right thing to do for their wellbeing. I have learned that the feelings I buried alive resurrected and overflowed, much to our detriment. In hindsight, I believe it would have been better for the boys to see me struggle and crumble a few times rather than be perceived as an unbreakable woman, which was certainly not the case. Even though more than a decade has passed since that horrible morning when I woke up to my new reality, sometimes I still cry when I'm alone. Those who know me well might be surprised because I am usually cheerful and happy, my grief does not define me. However, the sadness does not go away, I have just learned to live with it.

I had become a master at isolating my feelings and tucking them away to process at a later moment. I often used the word "numbness" because lack of feeling was a welcome respite to the intense hurt that often overwhelmed me. My level of grief was so crushing that I was acutely aware of the moment or the day I did not feel pain. It was difficult to get up, hard to get moving. The numbness allowed me to function. It was helpful for the most part, except when my sons needed less detachment and more of my presence. Along the way, I made this mistake and others, but considering the trauma of our circumstances, I'd like to think the boys emerged somewhat bruised but not broken, relatively unscathed. However, due to my life experiences, I now know that only time will tell.

Both Randy and I greatly benefited from our education, so the idea sending our sons off to college was an imperative that guided our parenting. To do so on my own was a daunting task and it felt impossibly far away, like a tiny glimmer of light in the dark tunnel of my early widowhood. It was visible, but I would have to walk treacherous miles to get there. I felt I had no choice but to equip the boys with the ability to provide for themselves. Getting an education was the only way I could envision of accomplishing that goal. As I tentatively walked through this tunnel, I realized I had to be in a good place to be a good mom. Otherwise, the obstacles were mental, spiritual and physical ... with many pitfalls in between.

Randy used to say, "If mom is happy, everyone is happy." This was definitely true. My first lesson was this: Do the best you can and forgive yourself if you mess up. Each day provided the opportunity to learn from your past mistakes. The important thing was to review at sunset and restart with each sunrise. Be kind and love yourself.

"Love your neighbor as thyself." Most people of faith focus on first part of this commandment—to love your neighbor. As a young woman, I found myself giving outwardly to my sons, my husband and my community. However, after Randy's death, I had to rein myself in and be mindful of loving myself.

My new circumstances forced me to pare down my existence to the bare minimum necessary—the boys and whatever was relevant to them. In the beginning, the only "me" activity I retained was exercising. It was crucial that I continued the discipline of working out because it provided the physical release, the bodily stamina and the mental decompression I needed to face the week ahead. Grief takes both an enormous emotional and physical toll on the body. Exercising not only kept me healthy but it also connected me with Dorothy, one of my new best friends. Life had thrown both of us several curveballs and shattered our glass castles. We bonded as kindred souls who cheered each other on while we crafted our new identity as single mothers. Friends are important, the old ones enveloped me in a protective cocoon and my new ones help me grow and evolve.

Being in a good place and loving myself also meant finding happiness in endeavors that extended beyond raising my sons. But how could I live a well-rounded life when everything was so lopsided? My purpose as the sole parent was fraught with sometimes joy, occasional pride and small satisfactions. It was also laced with emotions that could be depleting, filled with worries, exhaustion and unfairness. In an attempt to find balance, I developed a personal philosophy to discern what activities would merit their way into my life. I call this "Debbie's Three Es," which stand for Edifying (good for my soul), Entertaining (fun for me), and Economically Sensible (would it either make or save money?). When Randy died, my life was severely lacking in time and energy, so anything that I added had to accomplish at least two of the "Es." More often than not, it usually encompassed all three. Otherwise, said endeavor was a frivolous waste of my personal resources, something I could not afford nor juggle.

Obviously, this unwanted journey transformed me. My greatest personal change was learning to abandon the notion of control. To this day, I continue to remind myself to let go because my nature tends toward being controlling. I can't change who I am, but I can be mindful of my shortcomings. It was not easy to surrender the outcome of my circumstances to God's will, but Randy's demise unequivocally placed me on the path to learn this lesson. In the beginning, such was my loss that I really had no other choice. I was one breath away from imploding and collapsing. As I molted from my past and evolved into this new version of myself, I could acknowledge the help, guidance and support I was receiving from God. Even if I had less faith, the coincidences were simply too many to ignore. He patiently allowed my doubts and anger to abate while mercifully carrying our family forward. I had the choice to be grateful and trust that the Lord would care for us, or I could try to do it my way. I took a leap of faith and landed on what has been undeniably the easier and steadfast path.

Choosing faith brought much peace when confronting the very real obstacles that were on my journey. I learned to make the distinction between fear and concern. The first was depleting and debilitating, the latter was a call to action which once accomplished meant I could rest. "Your greatest fear in life is what you worship". This profound statement forced me to examine my deepest fears and to discern if such had become my gods: my children, our wellbeing, money, or my ego. In doing so, I made the conscious choice to place my relationship with God above everything. Happily, it has been a long while since I have felt the sinking and debilitating feeling of fear. The first commandment continues to guide me and gives me peace.

Regarding the inevitable concerns that come hand in hand with parenthood, trusting the Lord and "Leaving it in God's hands" also allowed me to breathe a sigh of relief when I was faced with the challenges of adolescence, financial worries, broken bones, injuries and second guessing some of my choices. It also helped me navigate the unexpected setbacks that are a normal part of life. With trust comes acceptance. "It is what it is" is the phrase my sons will probably associate with me as their mother for the rest of their lives.

Our holidays and special dates changed forever. I had to come to terms with this notion to create our new traditions and rituals for our truncated family. I also learned to pray for the right influences, male role models, coaches, etc. to make their way into my sons' life and afford them a view of what a normal family might look like. Leaving things up to God did not mean ignoring the problem or pretending there was none. Instead, it meant recognizing an issue, accepting that it was out of my hands, while having the faith that my prayers would be answered. It also meant acknowledging that the solution could be unconventional, surprising or perhaps not to my liking.

I've also acquired more empathy and an extra measure of patience. Again, these traits are not in my nature but having experienced the depths brought on by widowhood has allowed me a better understanding of what other people may be feeling at any given moment. That being said, after confronting problems that were insurmountable to most, I confess occasional irritation when people make a big deal about what I now consider trivial. Sometimes, I'm tempted to say, "Put on your big girl panties and move on." The impatient and pragmatic Hakka in me still shows up once in a while, so I have to remember to bite my tongue and maintain my poker face.

Grief erases any sense of normalcy, and it can make you do strange things. Therefore, I did not aspire to be normal because I was exploring just what my sons and I could consider "normal." I avoided saying, "I'm fine," because that was far from the truth. A better answer for me was, "As best as possible." I think most people appreciated my honesty and genuineness, because I stayed true to my actual feelings and circumstances. As time passed, I found that normal was a construct of my imagination.

250

Nothing in my situation could ever approximate normalcy. I realized that what I really sought all along was peace. It took me a while to acknowledge that normal no longer mattered, but peace was my holy grail which I sought as I related to my children, my surroundings, and my world.

For the widowed, solitude can be both a blessing and a curse. I could have given into a very real tendency to back away from life after Randy's death, but thankfully I am innately a social creature. Because of my children and new business, I remained connected to my community and was graced by the much-needed company and love of my friends and acquaintances. However, solitude with God was important because it was the only real way to unburden my soul, no one else could possibly fathom what was going on inside of me. Only my Creator could know every single one of my thoughts, fears and regrets. Only He could support me through this trial, breaking my useless circular ruminations, occupying a void that no one else could have filled.

Acknowledging my grief, my humanity and my weakness allowed me the openness to receive help from both my village and from my God. In asking for help, I also had to accept that asking was a new reality in my life. This was not an easy process because it forced me to confront my own ego and pride. It was also an opportunity for self-examination and introspection. In the end, I found that ego and fear were my greatest saboteurs while love and faith overdelivered.

Even after ten years, the garage is still as messy as Randy's studio was. I have taken my time to tidy up because some things are just no longer important. Once I was widowed, whatever bar I set with very high standards fell clanging to the floor. I was kind to myself and lowered my own expectations because just getting through the day was a big deal. Finishing the first year without falling apart was an achievement. Lowering the bar has been liberating, I am only accountable to my Maker and myself.

As noted in my story, I have a deep distrust of the pharmaceutical industry. This is not unfounded. In the 1990s Baxter was known as one of the best companies for working mothers. Everything in the manufacturing world revolved around saving and improving lives. I was part of the ethical side of the industry. Through my experience with Randy, I witnessed the darker side of big pharma, where corporate greed and profit decimated lives, including ours. As I embarked on the journey to tell this story, it would be fortuitous that my newest mentor provided some valuable insight into Randy's health conundrum.

I connected with Jack Watts, a brilliant and handsome man, through one of the many synchronicities that color my life with amazement. I was looking for some genuine feedback but none of my friends could possibly give me an unbiased opinion. One day, I was having a casual conversation with a business colleague and I randomly asked her if she knew an author. Surprisingly, she did. Her neighbor had written an award-winning memoir and over a dozen other books. She connected me with Jack and he agreed to read my first chapter. Jack saw the potential this story had to help others and he offered to become my mentor. Beyond the Breakpoint is truly the product of his guidance and our collaboration. Again, the Lord placed the perfect person (on many levels) in my path to bring this story to fruition.

Jack also provided an integral piece of the puzzle to Randy's health conundrum. At some point in his colorful life, he was a sales representative for the maker of the exact same muscle relaxants prescribed to Randy. He had knowledge that this medication could cause addiction, but the company actively hid this from the general public. Unexpectedly, he revealed to me a critical piece of Randy's health enigma. I never understood how he could succumb to the addiction after months of being "fine." Now I know that using muscle relaxants to deal with his back pain triggered a cascading chain of events that culminated in a crisis, his overdosing and the need for rehab. Randy was an unsuspecting victim of the pharmaceutical industry's drive for profits.

I had already moved forward not knowing what set Randy onto the road to relapse and I had learned to live with that unanswered question. Thanks to Jack, I finally have a better understanding of what my husband unwittingly battled and what initiated his downfall. Jack's knowledge did not change any outcomes nor the cognizance of my reality. However, this life altering information brought me further peace as it was proof that Randy's latter downfall and addiction resulted from the deceit of the drug makers and not a character flaw. My empathy for Randy broadened and I could better understand his torment.

I avoid thinking of the "what if" had we known better. It's a space I do not want to revisit because it no longer has any bearing. If I allowed myself to think of what might have been, my life could unravel in ways that no one wants to contemplate. There is nothing to gain by going down that corridor. I choose to be in awe of how this knowledge came to me and to be grateful for the additional serenity it brings.

My mistrust and concerns over big pharma, however, were justified. What Randy's health challenge taught me is that every medication has its downsides. There is no such thing as a magic bullet. There are side effects. Worse, in some cases these include addiction for the unfortunate who are genetically predisposed. I find it better to exhaust the holistic options before allowing modern medications to intervene.

The greatest takeaway that I hope to convey is the notion that I did not do this alone. Along with my parents and my brother, I had an entire village that supported us through this season of our lives. My friends helping hands, prayers, silent understanding or loud commiseration were an essential part of my quest from mourning to joy. They have my everlasting gratitude. It also took this incredible experience for me to fully acknowledge that I am a treasured child of God. Whenever I happen to see a "Jesus Loves You" bumper sticker, I think to myself "But I'm his favorite child". In all humbleness, HE never abandoned me. He provided for our family in countless and immeasurable ways. I owe our survival, my peace and the fact that my sons and I are thriving because of Him.

I hope this story is a testimonial of my own faith journey and an inspiration for others to seek their own relationship with God. These days I can look at my life through rose colored glasses because I am infinitely grateful for all that has transpired and for the lifelines from above. My husband is in heaven, I made it past the breakpoint, and my sons are excelling. What more could I hope for than this? Randy and I are where we need to be … and in peace.

The End

*I*n additional to her successful professional accomplishments as an engineer, image consultant and advertising content producer, Debbie also worked as Chief of Staff for the Dooner Group, a marketing consultancy firm. Continuing to give back to her community, she served as a trustee for the YMCA of the Palm Beaches and was the first woman to spearhead their Annual Fundraising Campaign. Debbie is actively launching her healthy lemongrass beverage to the market.

Debbie continues to play an active role in her three children's lives. David is soon to graduate as a Mechanical Engineer from Cornell University and Michael is pursuing a degree in Finance at Boston

College. Christian is in middle school, enjoying his role as the little Emperor – master of Debbie's universe.

Debbie's passion is helping people reach their fullest potential and advance after a life changing event. She continues to focus on life coaching, bereavement ministry, and is available upon request as inspirational speaker. Learn more by visiting her website at www.debbiefaris.com

Made in the USA
Monee, IL
12 March 2021